Are We Good Citizens?

AFFAIRS POLITICAL, LITERARY, AND ACADEMIC

Also By Harvey J. Kaye

The British Marxist Historians:
An Introductory Analysis (1984, new edition 1995).

History, Classes and Nation-States:
Selected Writings of V. G. Kiernan [1] (editor, 1988).

The Face of the Crowd:
Selected Essays of George Rudé (editor, 1988).

Poets, Politics and the People:
Selected Writings of V. G. Kiernan [2] (editor, 1989).

E. P. Thompson:
Critical Perspectives (editor, with Keith McClelland, 1990).

The Powers of the Past:
Reflections on the Crisis and the Promise of History (1991).

The Education of Desire:
Marxists and the Writing of History (1992).

The American Radical
(editor, with Mari Jo Buhle and Paul Buhle, 1994).

Imperialism and Its Contradictions:
Selected Writings of V. G. Kiernan [3] (editor, 1995).

Ideology and Popular Protest
by George Rudé (editor, 1995).

"Why Do Ruling Classes Fear History?" and Other Questions (1996).

Revolutionary Europe
by George Rudé (editor, 2000).

Thomas Paine:
Firebrand of the Revolution (2000).

Are We Good Citizens?

AFFAIRS POLITICAL, LITERARY, AND ACADEMIC

HARVEY J. KAYE

FOREWORD BY
Frances Fox Piven

Teachers College, Columbia University
New York and London

Published by Teachers College Press, 1234 Amsterdam Avenue, New York, NY 10027

Copyright © 2001 by Teachers College, Columbia University

All rights reserved. No part of this publication may be reproduced or transmitted in any form or by any means, electronic or mechanical, including photocopy, or any information storage and retrieval system, without permission from the publisher.

Library of Congress Cataloging-in-Publication Data
Kaye, Harvey J.
    Are we good citizens? : affairs political, literary, and academic / Harvey J. Kaye; foreword by Frances Fox Piven.
      p. cm.
    Includes bibliographical references and indexes.
    ISBN 0-8077-4020-9 (cloth)—ISBN 0-8077-4019-5 (pbk.)
    1. United States—Politics and government—1989–   2. United States—Intellectual life.
3. National characteristics, American.   4. Citizenship—United States—Philosophy.
5. Civil society—United States.   6. Democracy—United States.   7. Education, Higher—United States—Philosophy.   I. Title

E839.4.K39 2000
973—dc21

                                                                                                         00-051074

ISBN 0-8077-4019-5 (paper)
ISBN 0-8077-4020-9 (cloth)

Printed on acid-free paper

Manufactured in the United States of America

08 07 06 05 04 03 02 01   8 7 6 5 4 3 2 1

For good friends and their families
Carl, Kay, Richard, Tara, Catriona, and Rochelle Chinn
Tony, Janice, and Alex Galt
Jay, Lindi, Ben, and Aaron Kuritz
Craig, Kathy, Chris, and Colin Lockard

WITHDRAWN
UTSA LIBRARIES

Contents

Foreword by Frances Fox Piven ix
Acknowledgments xi
Introduction xiii

Affairs Political

1	God, Sex, and the Blues	3
2	The Emergence of Class Politics?	7
3	Dear Mr. President: A Plea for a Progressive Legacy	11
4	Conservative Chutzpah, Radical-Democratic Hopes	15
5	The People's Team: The Green Bay Packers —or The Super Bowl as Political Drama *with Isaac Kramnick*	19
6	FDR: A Great but Flawed President —or Visiting the New Memorial	25
7	Labor and the Intellectuals: A New Cultural Front?	28
8	Up-Ending the End of History, Redeeming America's Prophetic Memory	34
9	Getting Back Our Bite	40
10	1968–1998	44
11	1848 and All That—or A Vision of Poetry in Motion	47
12	The Third Way Is the Wrong Way	51
13	Signs of Life: American History, Memory, and Democracy	55

Affairs Literary

14	In Bookstores, Bigger Can Be Better	63
15	Reading the Right—or It's a Dirty Job, But ...	66
16	Writing for Kids—or In Praise of Juvenile Efforts	71
17	Are Americans More Inquisitive?	74
18	Send in the Historians—or The Yanks Are Coming Over There	77
19	Radical Ambivalence	80
20	Remembering and Honoring Our Fathers— or Democratic Generations	83
21	Fanning the Spark of Hope in the Past: The British Marxist Historians	87

Affairs Academic

22	Are We Good Citizens?	97
23	A Nation of Teachers	101
24	Starting All Over Again	106
25	Back in the Saddle, and Loving It: Post-Sabbatical Thoughts	112
26	Search for Sixties Soul	115
27	A Yank in London—or Love and Class Struggles	118
28	History and the Great Balloon Debate	122
29	The Nest Starts to Empty— or You Can See Her from Monticello	125
30	Collegial Pleasures	128
31	Felicity at the Barricades	131
32	Pilgrims with Tales to Tell	134
33	Turning 50 on the Eve of 2000	138
34	The Dialectic of Mentoring	141

Notes   *145*
Index   *157*

Foreword

Reading these wonderful essays reminded me of my visit to Green Bay, Wisconsin, a few years ago. Harvey Kaye had invited me to give a talk at the university, and I stayed at the Kaye home, where I met Lorna and daughters Rhiannon and Fiona. The essays made me smile at their warmth and buoyancy, and so did the unassuming and open-hearted Kaye household. Pictures of family, sometimes arm and arm with the greats of British Marxism, covered the refrigerator. Beer or pots of tea on hand, and good music in the background. Stacks of books and a mind-boggling array of journals and magazines tumbled everywhere. And Harvey was usually at my elbow, enthusiastically pointing out this or that article or book that I might have missed and must read immediately, and then putting together intimidating piles for me to take to bed.

These essays are like that weekend. Kaye is an intellectual, and a man of the left. He is widely erudite about history and theory, and also about sports and comics. But his keen observations about contemporary politics in Britain and the United States, about the state of the universities and the wonderful Green Bay Packers, his astute critiques of new important books, are not spoken by some unrooted authoritative voice. Rather Kaye always speaks his opinions in the first person, and he locates his arguments in the context of his own life. We know about where he was and what he was doing, about his daily worries and small triumphs, about how he feels about getting older or about his first daughter going off to college. He shows by example that intellectual life and political commitment is also a life of the concrete and personal.

Of course, what makes the warm context of the personal so striking and so welcome is the quality of these intellectual and political commentaries. They shine with the sheer joy of a life immersed in the intellectual and political traditions of the left. It is worth noting how unusual this is. Left intellectuals are often cranky, their writings conveying a deep pessimism and a sense of their own martyrdom to their commitments. Not Harvey Kaye. His is a sensibility that not only appreciates the intellectual and cultural traditions of the left, but enjoys, even revels, in those traditions and understands the manifold ways they have enriched his life.

Best of all, Kaye has a firm sense of why he writes. He thinks of himself as a public intellectual, and he writes with a clarity and verve that speaks directly to his readers. His public mission is profound. To paraphrase his words, he wants to cultivate and encourage our critical historical memory, our consciousness, and our imagination because, no matter the tragedies, our humanly created history has also yielded us at least some freedoms, some equality, and some justice. To cultivate our historical memory, in other words, is to fan the spark of hope for a better society on which the left depends.

Frances Fox Piven
Graduate Center
City University of New York

Acknowledgments

These pages afford me a chance to acknowledge debts, extend appreciations, and register affections. I must start by thanking Frances Fox Piven, whose work I so much admire, for honoring me with a Foreword to this book. Also, I want to thank David Jobbins at the *Times Higher Education Supplement* for licensing me to write so many of the pieces that make up this collection.

Closer to home, I want to thank my University of Wisconsin–Green Bay colleagues for putting up with my enthusiasms and contentiousness, and for regularly returning the compliment. I have in mind Tony Galt, Craig Lockard, Ron Baba, Jerry Rodesch, Dave Jowett, Lynn Walter, Kim Nielsen, Chris Terrien, Pam Schoen, Alison Kibler, Carol Emmons, Jeff Entwistle, and Mark Perkins.

A number of my students deserve special recognition for teaching me a thing or two—in particular, Carrie Cole, Annette Spakowicz, Tania Krall, Monica Depka, Maggie Gissal, Linda Gray, Mike Halberg, Julie Hardtke, Emily Johnson, Leah Kemp, Dave Lamers, Amy Malliett, Wayne Malone, Bryan Milz, Dave Peters, Cecil Roebuck, Ethan Shippert, Jeane Smits, Ryan Stockwell, and Jason Zimmer.

From Green Bay to Great Britain, friends have either helped me figure things out or created better problems to occupy my time. Elliott Gorn has never failed to instigate me. Cecelia Cancellaro has kept me connected to New York City. Tom Perry has joined me in bringing East Coast enthusiasms to northeast Wisconsin. Isaac Kramnick has given me more than one good idea. Carl Chinn has had the smarts to prove I know a winner when I see one. Helen and Denis Stevenson have provided a home away from home in London. Henry Giroux urged me to write about education. Steve Hein has talked with me about family and football. Harvey and Judy Medress have shared their Packer tickets with me. Chris Caldwell, though we line up on opposing sides, has advanced my thinking about politics. Steve Paulson has conferred with me about books. Matt Rothschild has asked me to write about several of them. And James Axtell suggested I create this one.

For enabling me to answer the question "Are we good citizens?" without too much shame or regret, I thank my fellow directors of the Wisconsin Labor History Society, especially Joanne Ricca, David Newby, Darryl Holter, Paul Cigler, Victor Greene, and Ken Germanson. And for having included me in the hard work, frustration, and solidarity that went into the co-founding of Scholars, Artists, and Writers for Social Justice (SAWSJ), I thank Nelson Lichtenstein, Steve Fraser, Michael Kazin, Margaret Levi, Ellen Schrecker, Joshua Freeman, Eileen Boris, and Paul Buhle.

Teachers College Press presented the opportunity for me to turn this collection of writings into a book. I thank Brian Ellerbeck for recruiting the volume, Carole Saltz for making it happen, and Carol Collins for working with me and seeing it through to publication. For allowing me to reprint the present essays I must also acknowledge the editors at *The Times Higher Education Supplement*, *The Capital Times*, *Tom Paine.com*, *Democratic Left*, *The Progressive*, *Rethinking History*, *The Review of Education*, *Pedagogy and Cultural Studies*, *Tikkun*, *The Chronicle of Higher Education*, and *The Washington Post*.

My family has always played a big part in my work, and I treasure their doing so. As former teachers, my parents-in-law, Anne and Lorimer Stewart, have perennially encouraged my professorial labors. My mom, Frances Kaye, has always supported and cheered my efforts. My sister and brother-in-law Phyllis and Bill Bauman have never failed to help in so many ways. And I would accomplish very little without my wife Lorna and our daughters Rhiannon and Fiona. I love them more than words can say.

Finally, I dedicate this volume to our good friends: the Chinn, Galt, Kuritz and Lockard families. They help make life ever richer.

Harvey J. Kaye
University of Wisconsin–Green Bay

Introduction

Are We Good Citizens? presents a collection of my writings on politics, ideas, books, and academic life. Given all the anxious talk we hear about citizenship in America, I should perhaps explain. When I speak of citizenship I do not have in mind good deeds, volunteerism, community service, or charitable acts—however essential, admirable, and worthy such things necessarily are in a society, and a world, perennially in need of caring and giving folk.

I understand citizenship in more historical, political, and democratic terms. I think about the radical promise of the Declaration of Independence and the Constitution. And I recall the words "all men are created equal . . . endowed by their Creator with certain unalienable Rights . . . among these are Life, Liberty and the pursuit of Happiness . . . " and "We the People of the United States, in Order to form a more perfect Union, establish Justice . . ."

I wonder, in particular, about my academic comrades' and my own intellectual labors. Have we become the citizen scholars we hoped to become? Have we—as C. Wright Mills urged us—critically applied our knowledge, skills, and imaginations to cultivating publics and enhancing our fellow citizens' capacities to exercise reason and freedom?[1] And, confronted with persistent and growing inequalities, concentrating power and wealth, and the ever-increasing threat they represent to democratic life and possibilities, what can we and should we do by way of our teaching, scholarship, and public engagements to redeem America's prophetic memory of liberty, equality, and democracy?

The question "Are we good citizens?" has troubled me all the more these past several years because of Americans' seeming lack of interest in politics and apathy about the nation's public prospects—circumstances that have led many a social scientist to speak of a crisis of American civil society (see Chapter 4). At times, it has even seemed as though conservative intellectual Francis Fukuyama was right when he argued that we had reached the "end of history"—that we were witnessing not only the welcome end of the Cold War, the collapse of Soviet Communism, and the triumph of liberal democracy but also the finale of world history. In a highly promoted 1989 article and, later, in *The End of History and the Last Man*, he audaciously asserted that we had reached the terminus of Western and world-historical development and that the present order of things represented the best of all possible worlds, beyond which the choice is either more of the same or economic and political retrogression.² In other words, we shouldn't hope, aspire, and seek to transform politics and society in a more profoundly democratic fashion, for it would be foolish, if not dangerous, to try to do so. We must accommodate ourselves to the present state of affairs.

Reading Fukuyama's claims with reference to power and ambition, we recognize that they stand in a long line of ruling elites' efforts to persuade those whom they rule that the way things are is the way they have to be. Throughout history upper classes and their hired hands have issued such pronouncements. Reading them more innocently, they seem no less outrageous, for they deny so much history and ignore the historical aspirations and creative agency of so many millions worldwide. In any case, they seem particularly, if not essentially, *un*-American. Founded in a great revolution, American history, for all its tragedy and irony, has entailed continual efforts and significant victories to extend and deepen freedom, equality, and democracy. And those movements and advances have imbued American experience with an enduring democratic impulse, however subdued that impulse may occasionally be. History has not come to an end. The struggle for democracy has not ceased.³

Admittedly, the chapters that follow do reveal my anxiety about the current state of American democratic life. Yet they also express my critical appreciation of America's continuing democratic possibilities, my unwavering confidence in my fellow citizens' democratic instincts, and my eager hope that intellectuals—professors and teachers alike—will recommit, or more strenuously commit, themselves to the reinvigoration of the nation's democratic impulse and the development of our capacities to realize its promise.

Though I may not have fully answered the question, and not every one of the following essays may evince it, "Are we good citizens?" has underlain the thinking that went into almost all of this work and motivated much of the writing. Contrary to the claims of our right-wing antagonists, the question has long challenged the student generation of the late 1960s.

Several of these chapters first appeared in such diverse places as *The Washington Post*, *The Chronicle of Higher Education*, *Tikkun*, *The Progressive*, *Democratic Left*, *Rethinking History*, and *The Review of Education/Pedagogy/ Cultural Studies*. But the majority originated as my contributions to "World View," the international column of *The Times Higher Education Supplement*

(THES), and I have drawn the book's title from the very first of those pieces (see Chapter 22).[4]

I had contributed articles, profiles, commentaries, diaries, and reviews to the THES on a fairly steady basis for almost ten years when, in the fall of 1994, David Jobbins, the foreign editor, asked if I would like to write as a World View columnist. I had always enjoyed writing for the paper. The prospect of doing a regular column thrilled me (for, to be honest, I had long aspired to just such a commission). I accepted the invitation as an honor and a challenge.

The World View column rotates weekly through a roster consisting of university chancellors, vice chancellors, deans, and professors from fairly distinguished institutions, from every corner of the globe. I myself had always viewed administrators with suspicion—not only because of an innate hostility to authority and strong labor sympathies but also because I could never figure out why anyone would give up teaching for management (aside from power and money, which hardly seemed reasons to respect such folk). Nevertheless, I recognized I would be joining a pretty distinguished cohort.

What really excited me, however, were the intellectual and political possibilities. I cannot deny that such an invitation from a major American publication would likely have elated me even more.[5] But my work on subjects like the British Marxist historical tradition and the politics of history and memory had taught me not to permit boundaries, national or intellectual, to limit my imagination too much.

I had written *The British Marxist Historians* and *The Education of Desire*, in part, to make the British tradition of radical history and ideas more accessible to scholars and students beyond the field of English history.[6] And I had written *The Powers of the Past* because I felt academics on both sides of the Atlantic had failed to fully appreciate the dangerous implications of the concurrent and connected rise of the British and American New Rights. Those movements possessed hegemonic ambitions. They had captured control of the British Conservative and American Republican parties in the 1970s, and soon after had ascended to governing power under the leadership of Margaret Thatcher and Ronald Reagan. Their ambitions both endangered many of our finest liberal and social-democratic achievements and promised to limit future democratic development. Especially, I wanted to call attention to their respective, but quite similar, uses and abuses of the past *and* their plans to reduce historical education to propagating the ideology of the "end of history."[7] I now hoped that my projected contributions to World View would serve to better inform international colleagues of American political, cultural, and educational developments, and—ever the student—that the experience of writing World View would train me for further, possibly American, public-intellectual endeavors.

Writing for the THES had advanced a somewhat different challenge than that of writing for scholarly journals or, for that matter, political magazines. The former entailed addressing myself not merely to those who shared a particular intellectual discourse, but, even more so, to readers who might have little or no familiarity with my topics and concerns, yet might want to (*or* at least might want to know if they should).

At the same time—for all the strain of composing transacademically *and* transatlantically (American does not always translate easily to English)—writing for the THES always seemed more natural than other kinds of "scholarship." It demanded a style of communication more akin to teaching (without being too pedantic), an activity that professors engage in almost daily.

Then, again, World View presented fresh challenges and possibilities. I had authored opinion pieces for American periodicals like *The Chronicle of Higher Education* and *Education Week*.[8] For better or worse, I had never failed to have opinions. Growing up in New York's Jewish culture had imbued me with a critical voice and a love of argument. There's a fair bit of truth in the saying "talk to two Jews, you'll get three opinions." Not to mention, I take the term *professor* seriously. Now I would have regular, guaranteed opportunities to report, reflect, journalize, *and* editorialize on American experience.

Of course, I knew that the editors at the THES intended the World View column for reportage and commentary on *academic* developments and that my co-contributors usually limited their pieces to institutional matters. But I didn't assume I would have to strictly follow suit. Fortunately, my editor didn't expect me to. Well aware of my political and cultural commitments, David Jobbins stipulated only that my contributions should "relate" to higher education. That allowed for a lot of latitude, and I interpreted my commission broadly. How could I not? The very scale of American higher education, and its extensive presence in our national life, required me to do so.

Motivated by democratic values, the campaigns of my own student generation had helped to undermine the barriers dividing the academy from the "real world." Yet we were hardly the worst culprits. In the wake of the long and tumultuous sixties (though, perhaps, not long or tumultuous enough), New Right politicians and their cadres of corporately endowed public intellectuals had laid siege to academe. They had sought through their pursuit of the culture wars to counter our accomplishments and subject American scholarship and teaching to conservative and corporate priorities. They may not have vanquished the academic Left, but their incessant attacks definitely contributed to the further subjection of collegiate culture to capitalist norms, values, and practices.

I considered dedicating all of my columns to the continuing threat that New Right ambitions posed to higher education and public culture. But, as compelling as that seemed (especially as I would get to do so in the pages of a newspaper owned by none other than the conservative, global-media mogul Rupert Murdoch), I worried that after a while it would bore even the most politically committed. Moreover, although the 1994 "Gingrich Revolution" had revived the culture wars, those particular battles appeared to wane in the wake of the 1996 elections. In fact, other developments—most especially in the American labor movement—began to raise the real possibility of revitalizing progressive politics (see Chapter 7). Increasingly, I saw my column writing as a means of highlighting or bearing witness to the beginnings of American democratic renewal. Also, as new opportunities presented themselves to contribute to various American periodicals, I hoped my writing would further encourage that process.

As well as resolving to write for the THES in a more "political" fashion than did my fellow contributors, I decided to allow myself to write in a more autobiographical mode. We Americans have a reputation for brashness and, also, for openness. I expect my columns have reinforced such views of us. To give life to theory and abstraction, I had always drawn on personal experiences in my teaching. I naturally projected that practice into my columns.

By recounting my experiences as a student, professor, and parent of college-bound daughters, I have tried to provide a more intimate, down-to-earth, grassroots perspective on American academic life. And while I didn't want to discount the problems, I did want—after so many years of continuing gloom and doom in higher education—to remind colleagues of the persistent "pleasures of academe" and, thereby, encourage them to work to defend those relationships and experiences (see the Affairs Academic chapters, in particular). In that vein, I cannot help but note that whereas my American co-contributors to the THES write from large, prestigious, research-oriented universities (precisely Harvard and Berkeley), I write from a much smaller, (lower-salaried) teaching-oriented, undergraduate institution.

It may sound naively humanistic to say that in relating my own experiences I do not seek to elevate or celebrate them, but to share them and connect with others in the process. Indeed, I have found that my most autobiographical pieces or memoirs usually generate the greatest responses, instigating people to let me know how certain episodes reminded them of their own experiences and, sometimes, made them think about them in new ways. Don't storytellers seek to express the universal through the particular? (I took it as a compliment when one of the publisher's reviewers of this collection envisioned the work serving as a "stocking stuffer" for academics.)

I wanted my writing, both for the THES and for the American periodicals where I published similar work, to convey the persistent contradictions *and* the persistent possibilities of American life. Business and corporate opportunities receive plenty of attention. I wanted to highlight the *democratic* ones. Thus, one will find here considerations of American memory and imagination, America's radical tradition, the renewal of a labor–intellectual alliance, the embryonic activism of students, pedagogical practices to encourage democratic development, and even how the unique community-ownership arrangement of the Green Bay Packers football team represents an alternative to the "traditional" capitalist model.

I have chosen not to present the essays in chronological order. Instead, I have structured the work in terms of three themes: politics, books, and academic life. The first section, Affairs Political, includes chapters on national politics, public discourse, intellectuals, history, memory, class, community, capitalism, and the grand old question "What is to be done?" The second, Affairs Literary, consists of chapters on bookstores, reading, writing, narratives, and historiography. And the third, Affairs Academic, offers chapters on education, student life (past and present), teaching, parenting, and professorial anxieties and joys. Having organized the volume in this manner, I should point out that the respective themes do not stay discretely in place; to some extent, all three run through all three sections.

Bringing the pieces together as chapters, I have not removed, revised, or amended any of their arguments. However, I have taken the liberty of excising redundant remarks, restoring lines I had to jettison in order to meet the prescribed lengths, providing references, and adding postscripts where I thought it necessary or worthwhile. Also, for the sake of clarity, I have converted "English" words and expressions back to "American." (For example, I have changed the British "dons" to the American "academics," for—however powerful a presence some of our professorial ilk may possess—the former have nothing to do with "Godfathers.")

I could not possibly close this Introduction without referring to my political and intellectual hero, the great eighteenth-century revolutionary, Thomas Paine.[9] Recognizing Americans' possibilities, Paine, in his aptly titled *Common Sense* (1776), enabled his newly embraced fellow countrymen to see themselves not as subjects but as citizens. He appreciated their growing, but unspoken, aspirations for independence, and he proceeded to articulate those aspirations as a shared, compelling vision. We should try to emulate that kind of democratic radicalism.

Are We Good Citizens?

AFFAIRS POLITICAL, LITERARY, AND ACADEMIC

*Affairs
Political*

Chapter 1

GOD, SEX, AND THE BLUES

In contrast to the making of Thatcherite conservatism in Britain, the development and advance of the New Right in the United States has depended greatly on the formation and energy of a new evangelical politics. Whether the issue has been school prayer, abortion, gay rights, or cinematic sex and violence, religious arguments have been central to the American conservatives' "culture wars." Moreover, in the past few years this new Christian Right has succeeded in returning to the public agenda the grand question of the role of religion in civic and public affairs.

Such things are not exactly new to American experience. As Ronald Thiemann, Dean of Harvard's Divinity School, attests in his new book, *Religion in Public Life: A Dilemma for Democracy*, since earliest colonial times the role of religion in government and the larger realm of civil society continually has been a contentious matter.[1]

In fact, as historians Isaac Kramnick and R. Laurence Moore ably remind us in their new book, *The Godless Constitution*, to secure freedom of religious expression, and the independence of both the state and the several churches *from each other*, the Founding Fathers not only composed a secular and irreligious document, they also opened the very first amendment of the Bill of Rights with the words "Congress shall make no law respecting an establishment of religion, or prohibiting the free exercise thereof." Admittedly, doing so hardly resolved the issue. Nevertheless, the Founders themselves—a good many of whom were deists, like Thomas Jefferson—clearly intended to provide for the *separation* of church and state.[2]

Of course, the constitutional divorce of church and state did not mean that religion itself would cease to be an active presence in American public culture (nor did the Founders intend it to have such an effect). Thus, that great observer of American life, Alexis de Tocqueville, would write in 1835: "Upon my arrival in the United States, the religious aspect of the

---

Originally appeared in *The Times Higher Education Supplement*, May 31, 1996.

country was the first thing that struck my attention." Visitors today probably have the same reaction. Based on church membership and belief in a "Supreme Being," it is arguable that after 160 years Americans are not only *more* religious than they were, but also more religious than most other peoples are. (This is not to say that we are more moral than we were, or more moral than other folks are.)

The religious right—overwhelmingly composed of Protestant fundamentalists—was originally mobilized for Reagan Republicanism by the Reverend Jerry Falwell and his now-defunct Moral Majority movement. Yet today the foremost organization of the religious right is the Christian Coalition. Godfathered by televangelist and one-time presidential candidate Pat Robertson (whose key writings are apocalyptic and reminiscent of the anti-Semitic "Protocols of the Elders of Zion"), the Christian Coalition is led by the boyish-looking—but politically astute—Ralph Reed. Like Newt Gingrich, Reed holds a Ph.D. in history, which apparently makes him feel entitled to do with and to the past what he pleases.

The Christian Coalition learned from its early failures. Robertson himself seemed too ready to scrap the First Amendment and officially declare America a "Christian nation," thereby antagonizing too many good folk. Under Reed's leadership, it now trains "stealth" candidates for public office and downplays the specifically Protestant fundamentalist character of the organization by promoting itself as an ecumenical "pro-family" movement.

In his writings—most notably, his book *Politically Incorrect* (1994) and the Christian Coalition's *Contract with the American Family* (1995)—Reed repeats the litany of New Right politicians: reduce taxes; shrink government; privatize public broadcasting and the national endowments for the arts and humanities; and allow public dollars to fund private, religious, and parochial schools! But Reed puts a special religious spin on it.[3]

Ignoring the immense power of capital, and its subordination of social relations and morality to the values of the market, Reed insists that since the 1960s government, education, and the media have been taken over by left-liberal forces whose policies and programs have been both anti-religious and anti-family. Furthermore, he claims that liberals have been persecuting "people of faith" by perverting the Founders' intentions and using the constitutional principle of separation of church and state to drive religion and the faithful from "the public square." Dressing himself in the language of the Constitution, he urges passage of a "religious freedom amendment."

Reed's supporters include not only Republican presidential candidates like Bob Dole and Pat Buchanan, but, as well, leading conservative public intellectuals like William Bennett (a practicing Catholic, Ph.D. in philosophy, former head of the National Endowment for the Humanities, former Secretary of Education, and, presently, Cultural Policy Fellow at the Heritage Foundation, co-director of the Empower America organization, and editor of the massive bestsellers, *The Book of Virtues* and *Children's Book of Virtues*).[4]

While God only knows if they will ultimately succeed in their ambitions to subject public policy to fundamentalist religious direction, Reed and his cohort clearly have reshaped public debate. Of course, they may get more than they had bargained for.

Reflecting fresh thinking on the part of the political left, the liberal *Washington Monthly* ran a feature by Amy Waldman outlining "Why We Need a Religious Left"; and the progressive magazine *The Nation* ran a similar piece by renowned Harvard theologian Harvey Cox. Moreover, in works like *Jewish Renewal* by Michael Lerner, *The Soul of Politics* by Catholic activist Jim Wallis, and *Keeping Faith* by African American theologian Cornel West, liberals, progressive-populists, and radicals have begun to redeem a prophetic politics of the left.[5] And, addressing the upcoming 1996 presidential and congressional campaigns, this spring in Washington, D.C., will be held what promises to be an impressive "National Summit on Ethics and Meaning," organized by Lerner's magazine, *Tikkun*, Wallis's magazine, *Sojourners*, and a host of other progressive religious groups.

Universities themselves, whether religious or secular in foundation, have not been immune to the resurgence of religious politics. So far, it appears that conservative religious fervor and organizing, at least at the major public universities, have been limited to evangelical students and the likes of the Inter-Varsity Christian Fellowship (whose athletic members can regularly be seen huddling in prayer before and after sporting events).

However, courses on religion are reportedly growing in popularity nationwide; scholarly presses are searching eagerly for religious studies (W. B. Eerdmans, a leading publisher of such works, is thriving as never before); and, in books like George M. Marsden's *The Soul of the American University*, Warren Nord's *Religion and American Education*, and Mark Schwehn's *Exiles from Eden*, there have been serious calls to reintroduce faith into American intellectual and academic life. As Alan Wolfe writes in a recent issue of *Lingua Franca*: "Intellectual fashions being what they are, the next major issue facing higher education may well be the revival of religious faith."[6]

Finally—however much Reed and his ilk would disavow having had any influence—I cannot help but note that the feature story in the spring 1996 "College Issue" of *Rolling Stone* magazine also reflected the new attention being accorded to matters of faith. Treating the singer of the hit single "One of Us," which envisions God being just an everyday guy—with the singer herself smiling broadly and displaying proudly her ring-pierced nose on the magazine's front cover—the banner lines read: "Joan Osborne: Saved by God, Sex and the Blues."[7] Now, that's a religion I imagine a lot of students could subscribe to.

Chapter 2

THE EMERGENCE OF CLASS POLITICS?

In the months following the 1994 elections it became increasingly apparent that Republican successes represented not an advance for popular aspirations but, rather, another political victory for what historian and social critic Christopher Lasch cleverly called the "revolt of the elites."[1] And yet, just as a revolt of the nobility instigated the French Revolution, it is possible that this new rebellion from above will have served as the catalyst for resurgent struggles from below in 1990s America. Ironically, instead of securing a new conservative regime, the New Right's "Contract with America" seems to have engendered a new language, perhaps even a new politics, of *class*, offering critical possibilities for a politics of meaning.

America has always been a class-structured society, and the progress of democratic life regularly has entailed class conflict, quite often bloodier than in the supposedly more class-ridden European states. Nevertheless, another exceptional feature of our history has been the "myth of classlessness." Revised as the country developed, it continually has projected an image of the nation in which opportunities and mobility were so great as to effectively inhibit the formation of an Old World–style social structure. Admittedly, the myth's most recent rendition concedes that America actually is a class society; but, of course, it conceives of almost every American as "middle class."

In spite of radical historians' best efforts to reveal the class character of the American experience, the assumption that "we're all middle class" has persisted, at least in the rhetoric of politicians. Indeed, it is arguable that America's most taboo subject has been not religion, not race, no, not even sex, but, rather, class.

Whether due to repression or suppression, the persistent public denial of class has been all the more remarkable in the face of 20 years of "class war from above." The politics of Reaganism accelerated the process whereby the rich get richer and working people and the poor get

---

Originally appeared in *Tikkun*, vol. 11, no. 5, September/October 1996.

poorer. Yet the renewal of a political economy of increasing inequality really started in the mid 1970s, when Fortune 500 companies abandoned the postwar social contract and commenced an assault on workers and the labor movement not seen since the Depression.

Still, with leveraged buyouts and tax cuts for the rich, it is the eighties that truly deserve the designation "decade of greed." While corporate greed ruined lives and devastated communities, the powerful accumulated *and* celebrated wealth, certainly arousing class sensibilities. Television shows like *Dallas*, *Dynasty*, and *Lifestyles of the Rich and Famous* entertained, but they also reminded working people of the growing social divide.

As inequality grew and *Roseanne* became a hit comedy series, politicians and pundits continued to speak in terms of a grand middle class. However, by the end of the decade the term meant something different than it had before. Less and less, it referred to society as a whole; more and more, it became a rallying cry for working people. In *The Politics of Rich and Poor*, former Republican strategist Kevin Phillips warned of the growing concentration of wealth and the threat it posed to a strapped "middle class."[2] "New Democrat" Bill Clinton campaigned on the promise of addressing the erosion of "middle-class" living standards and prospects. And, strangely enough, conservatives themselves contributed to the spread of class thinking. Compelled to offer alternatives to race- and gender-based affirmative action, right-wing propagandists, such as Dinesh D'Souza, proposed *class*-based programs.[3]

The disappointments of the Clinton administration heightened the rising class awareness. Ignoring labor unionists' and environmentalists' pleas, the president and his cabinet colleagues fought harder for the North American Free Trade Agreement (NAFTA) and the General Agreement on Tariffs and Trade (GATT) than for any of the promised initiatives favoring labor and working families. Encountering opposition, they even abandoned their essentially pro-corporate plan for national healthcare, arrived at after long, secretive deliberations. In the same period, "downsizing" and the "decline of the middle class" became household expressions.

A popular sense of betrayal led to Democratic defeats in 1994. However, for all of the Republicans' expressions of concern for middle-income folk, their legislative schemes and deference to corporate lobbyists readily exposed the GOP for what it is, the party of big business and the well-off.

In 1994–95, "class talk" has broken out all over. *The New York Times* has issued special reports on the personal and collective consequences of "Downsizing in America," and the *Washington Post* has featured articles like "The Rich Get Richer and . . ."[4] Foundation-sponsored studies, such as Edward Wolff's *Top Heavy*, have inventoried the nation's increasingly gross wealth and income disparities, and more analytical works, like David

Gordon's *Fat and Mean*, have shown how they are a consequence of corporate agencies. In fact, whereas the neoconservative *American Enterprise* has produced a predictable special issue anxiously attempting to deny it all, the more influential *Business Week* has described in a cover story how workers are suffering a "wage squeeze" despite the robustness of corporate profits.[5]

Contrary to the Republicans' ambitions, their triumphs not only have expedited the emergence of class thinking, but also they have led to its refashioning. Apparently the term "middle class," no longer able to adequately accommodate the diverse experiences of professionals and managers *and* industrial and service workers, has given way to "middle class" and "working class," respectively. Early in 1995, the liberal magazine *American Prospect* published an article considering the evidence that much of the so-called middle class actually thinks of itself as "working class." The neoliberal *Washington Monthly* ran a cover piece urging the revival of the labor movement. And in a cover article, "Workers and the World Economy," *the* Establishment journal, *Foreign Affairs*, registered serious apprehension about the dangers of intensifying class inequalities and ferment.[6]

Additionally, I cannot help but note the appearance of the television series *Malibu Shores*, promoted as "the story of high school students from opposite sides of the track—the elite community of Malibu and the working-class San Fernando Valley." Public discourse has begun to more clearly reflect America's social structure.

Moreover, not just radicals, but now even vital-centrists, like Michael Lind, Kevin Phillips, and Jacob Weisberg, have taken to writing books projecting a class-based progressive politics.[7] Yet we should not be too sanguine. So far, the most evident political manifestation of a "class discourse" has been in Pat Buchanan's presidential campaign. Buchanan's rhetoric and appeal revealed the anger of working people (especially white workingmen) and sent shivers up the spines of corporate and conservative elites (who shamelessly responded with charges of "class warfare"). However, it also exposed strains of racism, anti-Semitism, sexism, and homophobia that will have to be addressed by any new progressivism.

At the same time, we have reason to be hopeful and active. Most importantly, the labor movement has started to resurrect itself. The AFL-CIO recently elected fresh, energetic leadership and made organizing its highest priority. Particularly notable here is "Union Summer," which, in the spirit of the civil rights movement's Freedom Summer, recruited and deployed 1500 students to workplace and community organizing drives in over a dozen cities. Also noteworthy is the upcoming "National Teach-In" scheduled for early October in which academics and intellectuals on campuses across the country will be speaking in solidarity with labor. Plus, the recent formation of a Labor party by several major unions, representing more than a million workers, should send the Democrats a direct message not to take organized labor for granted.

The emergence of class thinking and politics presents a real test to those seeking to develop a truly progressive politics. The challenge is to articulate a diverse cross-class alliance capable of engaging and advancing the democratic imaginations and prospects of both the middle and working classes, while insisting especially on the material and political empowerment of the latter.

Chapter 3

DEAR MR. PRESIDENT:
A PLEA FOR A PROGRESSIVE LEGACY

Dear Mr. President,

Inviting your fellow citizens to join you in "building a bridge to the twenty-first century," you won a remarkable reelection victory in 1996 and became the first Democrat since Franklin Roosevelt to secure a second full presidential term. You are now recomposing your cabinet and making plans for your new administration. No doubt, you are also wrestling with the grander historical question of what your presidential legacy ought to be and how you might yet determine it—a task made all the more complicated by a Republican Congress.

In hopes of securing some kind of legislative package, and a favorable place in the history texts, you will find it tempting to accept pundits' tales and counsels urging moderation, compromise, and centrism. Yet, before you do, I would ask you to entertain an alternative reading of recent political history and the possibilities it affords. Contrary to dictating "governing from the center," I believe recent developments actually present you with a critical opportunity to advance the nation in a far more progressive direction.

In January 1993, having successfully campaigned as a progressive and populist, you stood before the American people and asked us to "be bold, embrace change, and share the sacrifices needed for the nation to progress." I well recall how you summoned up the memory of the patriot and president, Thomas Jefferson, by retracing his inaugural trek from Monticello to Washington and by drawing upon his words for your own address. Your pronounced desire to restore and extend America's democratic imagination and agency moved many of us. However, when you proceeded to state that "Thomas Jefferson believed that to preserve the very foundations of

---

Originally appeared in *The Capital Times* (Madison, WI), 20 January 1997.

our nation, we would need dramatic change from time to time," you startled me and suppressed the very sense of hope and optimism you had begun to arouse.

After a dozen years of the New Right's politics of greed, division, and growing inequality, change was imperative. What disturbed me was not the prospect of change; it was what you had done to Jefferson's words and what your doing so portended.

Until that moment, it seemed that a truly democratic conception of politics inspired your campaign and that you had every intention of actually engaging and empowering the publics who had supported you. But the manner in which you invoked Jefferson's words suddenly indicated otherwise. As we both know, Jefferson didn't speak merely of "change." He spoke in more radical terms than that. Appreciating the legacy and promise of the Revolution, he said: "I hold that a little *rebellion* now and then is a good thing, and as necessary in the political world as storms in the physical." Your historical revision revealed an elitist, governing-class notion of politics and social change, if not actually a dread of the popular and democratic forces your own campaign had begun to awaken.

I didn't doubt your determination to pursue the changes you had promised, but I now fearfully foresaw that you—and we—were destined to fail. Success demanded more than election victories and more than your best intentions. It required committed and organized popular support. In the absence of a progressive movement to propel you forward, or a willingness on your part to work to foster its growth and development, it became tragically clear we would never be able to overcome the accumulated resources of the right and turn back their class war from above.

Predictably, and sadly, defeats and disappointments ensued. You scaled back your plans to rehabilitate America's infrastructure, and yet even the downsized version was rejected by a still-then Democratic Congress. Pursued in a starkly elitist fashion, your administration's endeavors to create a system of universal healthcare mobilized powerful corporate and professional forces in opposition, and the project came to a dead end. And, against the will of the labor and environmental movements that had supported you, you energetically and successfully sought passage of free-trade agreements. The Republicans' 1994 victories had far more to do with popular disappointment in your presidency than with any "Gingrich Revolution."

You grasped that and—though you irresponsibly signed the so-called Welfare Reform Act (which you now promise to amend and improve)—you fought your way back by defending Medicare and Medicaid, public education, the EPA and OSHA, affirmative action, the national endowments for the arts and humanities, and the public broadcasting system. Moreover, with the support of labor and a diverse coalition of progressive groups, you secured an increase in the minimum wage. Indeed, in the process of defending those programs, you and your Democratic colleagues further revealed the Republicans for what they are, proponents of corporate interests and right-wing extremism.

Your 1996 campaign may have lacked the verve and vision of 1992, but, significantly, your words and proposals professed a persistent concern for working people and their families and a desire to renew the nation's democratic impulse. Thus, the American people rejected a candidate whose party's platform and ambitions promised to place the commonwealth even more firmly in the hands of the well-off and the narrow-minded, and granted you a second chance to undertake the political and social changes you originally articulated. In fact, more has changed since 1992 than your margin of victory. Ironically, though legislative obstacles have increased, you may be more critically positioned now than you were four years ago, for the makings of a new progressivism have begun to take shape.

As *Washington Post* columnist E. J. Dionne appreciated, we only looked dead. Stirred by your first campaign, antagonized by your failures, shocked by conservative victories, and, perhaps, instigated anew by your reelection campaign, progressives have begun to move and to organize. Most significantly, American labor elected new leadership, committed to progressive politics and organizing the unorganized. Moreover, labor's resurgence has engendered a new campus activism among students and faculty. Far belying their reputation as "the last intellectuals," liberal and left professors across the country have been staging "teach-ins" in support of the labor movement.

At the same time, a diverse group of activists and intellectuals has organized the Campaign for America's Future; political insurgencies on the left of the Democratic party have led to the formation of the Labor party and the New party; and—in reply to the Christian Right's hijacking of religion and "family values"—progressive religious folk, Christian and Jewish, have gathered around a new "politics of meaning." Apparently, one of Jefferson's envisioned and welcomed "rebellions" is commencing.

Undeniably, there are matters requiring urgent attention and legislative action, making it imperative that you find a way of working with the Republican-dominated Congress. In such circumstances, the reconstitution of the "vital center" is itself a significant challenge and an honorable ambition. And yet, you are presented with a historic opportunity.

If you have it in you—to cite your own words—to be bold and embrace change—that is, if you are now prepared to engage the emerging progressive politics—then we can begin to pursue the revitalization of America's democratic development and redeem our shared aspirations. What is your legacy to be?

Sincerely,
Harvey J. Kaye

Chapter 4

CONSERVATIVE CHUTZPAH, RADICAL-DEMOCRATIC HOPES

What *chutzpah*! After two decades of New Right ascendance, conservatives have put the question—"Is American Democracy Dying?"—at the top of their political agenda. Posed most recently on the cover of *National Review*, it has been asked repeatedly in conservative publications this past year (1996). However exasperating it is, those of us committed to redeeming America's democratic impulse should attend carefully to this new conservative discourse. Ironically enough, the right's newly pronounced anxiety about the nation's democratic prospects may actually be—for reasons other than we might at first think—cause for hope.

The question of democracy's health is hardly original. Noting, among other things, the high cost of campaigns, the power of corporate contributions, the manipulation of the media, the superficiality of public debate, and the apathy of voters, liberal and progressive writers for some time now have been addressing the sorry state of American politics and civil society. Robert D. Putnam's celebrated article, "Bowling Alone," is not alone in describing the disappearance of the associational and civic-minded citizenry celebrated in Alexis de Tocqueville's *Democracy in America*. Other works on the subject abound: for example, E. J. Dionne's *Why Americans Hate Politics*; William Greider's *Who Will Tell the People?*; Lewis Lapham's *The Wish For Kings*; and Jean Bethke Elshtain's *Democracy On Trial*—not to mention the many anxious contributions to journals like *The American Prospect*, *Dissent*, and *Tikkun*.[1]

The question has become all the more urgent in the face of nasty rightwing talk-radio shows, armed militia groups, the Oklahoma City bombing, and the torching of African American churches. One feels compelled to restate Franklin Roosevelt's warning that "if American democracy ceases to move forward as a living force . . . fascism will grow in the land."

Originally appeared in *Democratic Left*, vol. 24, no. 5, November 1996. Reprinted by permission of Democratic Socialists of America.

Whatever the results of November's elections, the 1996 races have done little to assuage such concerns. Referring to the defeat of campaign-finance reforms, the cover of the summer issue of *Dollars and Sense* sadly, but rightly, announced "Democracy for Sale." Also treating the money issue, but at street level, a *New York Times* front-page story reported how campaign volunteers have given way to "hired hands" motivated not by ideology but, rather, by "a weekly paycheck whose size turns on the number of signatures they collect." And, of course, the August party conventions provided still further evidence of America's apparent political enervation. As a *New Republic* cover sarcastically proclaimed: "The One Thing America's Rich and Poor Share: An Indifference to Politics."[2]

That conservatives have posed the question of democracy's mortality, as well, hardly seems remarkable. However, to fully appreciate its significance we need to start by recognizing that the question is being asked universally on the right, by traditional, neo-, and paleo-conservatives alike.

In October 1995, the formerly liberal, but now conservative, social science magazine *Society* arranged a symposium on "The Future of Liberal Democracy." In November 1995, *Commentary*, the standard-bearer of neoconservatism, celebrated its fiftieth anniversary by asking 72 of its fellow-travelers to respond to the statement: "In the eyes of many observers, the United States, which in 1945 entered upon the postwar era confident in its democratic purposes and serene in the possession of a common culture, is now, fifty years later, moving toward balkanization or even breakdown."

Soon after, in January 1996, the handsomely endowed Heritage Foundation added *"The Journal of American Citizenship"* to the title of its popular magazine, *Policy Review*. The editors stated they did so to better communicate their new mission: "to restore the tradition of American citizenship by repairing the institutions of civil society and returning to the core political principles of our Founding Fathers." Next, *Chronicles*, the magazine of the paleo-conservative Rockford Institute, organized its July issue around the apprehensive theme "Virtual Democracy." And, again, the September 16th cover of *National Review*, the foremost magazine of political conservatism, asked, "Is American Democracy Dying?"

Moreover, as anxious as the "diverse" factions of the New Right have always been—about the crisis of education, the future of the literary canon, political correctness, multiculturalism, welfare mothers—it has been quite a while since they have universally concerned themselves with questions "democratic."

Yet we should not too eagerly assume that conservatives have realized the need to defend and enhance American democratic life. Let us not forget that the New Right itself originally took shape in hostile reaction to the "democratic surge" of the long 1960s and rose to power financially empowered by elements of corporate capital intent upon repelling social- and radical-democratic advances.

After so many leftist defeats and retreats—from the ERA to Clinton's signing of the so-called Welfare Reform Bill—and in the shadow of continuous conservative efforts to rewrite the history of the times, it may be difficult to recall how the struggles *and* achievements of the sixties for racial and gender equality, public action to combat poverty and hunger, ending the war in Southeast Asia, environmental protection, and workplace reforms were, in their respective ways, movements to extend and deepen American *democratic* life and practices. However, the powers that be well understood it and foresaw, perhaps more so than we did ourselves, that if the several movements ever came together in solidarity, even greater democratic changes would be forthcoming.

Echoing the fears of the corporate and political elites who sponsored it and the neoconservative intellectuals who authored it, the 1975 Trilateral Commission Report, *The Crisis of Democracy*, nervously declared that America was suffering from "an excess of democracy" due to the heightened political consciousness and activism of "public-interest groups, minorities, students, women, white-collar unions [and] value-oriented university and media intellectuals." Democracy had to be subdued and, fortunately for the corporate class, the Reagan Republicans were mobilizing even further to the right. The rest is history—or, as the conservatives would like all of us to concede, the *"end* of history."[3]

A generation later, the conservatives' renewed concern about democracy should not be mistaken for a change of heart. Not only do their writings evidence no sense of either responsibility or regret for what has transpired since, but the culprits in the tales they tell remain liberals and leftists—as Robert Bork's new book, *Slouching Towards Gomorrah: Modern Liberalism and American Decline*, testifies.[4]

Neglecting entirely the tyranny of growing corporate power and a liberated and expansive market economy, conservatives continue to attack "big government" and the likes of schoolteachers and their unions. Refusing to acknowledge the contradictions between market values and family values, they persist in warning about "radical egalitarianism." And, ignoring or abusing the memory of the struggles from below to enlarge both the "we" in "We, the people" and the process by which *we*, the people, can govern, they continue to insist that the answer to the nation's divisions and ills is renewed "civic virtue" and "religious fervor." Conservative ambitions remain that of limiting and constraining democratic aspirations and agencies.

At the same time, I think there is more to the new conservative discourse about democracy than merely the calculated and cynical manipulation of American history and values. Twenty years ago conservatives appreciated the democratic promise of the struggles of the day and successfully mobilized against them. Given the record, we should allow that, between us, the conservatives have been the more politically perceptive; and experience should tell us to take their anxieties and pronouncements seriously.

Though I very much doubt that conservatives fear the imminent demise of American democracy, I do wonder if their recent words shouldn't be read as a sign that they have started to sense a more familiar danger. Maybe the right and its corporate backers do have good reason once again to worry. Perhaps—in developments like the popular revulsion against the "Gingrich Revolution" and the revitalization of the labor movement, *plus* a host of other stirrings on the left—conservatives have begun to perceive the resurgence of America's historic democratic impulse.

It doesn't radically change things if they do, for, whatever is happening, our task of cultivating liberty, equality, and democratic community remains as demanding as ever. Yet, just maybe, we have even more reason to be hopeful that, in solidarity, liberals, progressives, and democratic socialists can engage that impulse and make it, once again, an imperative.

Chapter 5

THE PEOPLE'S TEAM:
THE GREEN BAY PACKERS—
OR THE SUPER BOWL AS POLITICAL DRAMA

with Isaac Kramnick

Public ownership got some surprisingly good copy during this past winter (1996–97) in, of all places, big-time sports, that bastion of competitive individualism and all-around gung-ho Americanism. After decades, when all one heard were the virtues of privatization, the media were seriously touting tales of nonprofit community-based enterprises right in the heartland of America, in "cheesehead" northeast Wisconsin.

The Super Bowl encounter between the New England Patriots and the Green Bay Packers in New Orleans for the National Football League championship warranted all the attention it received. The media hype, the column inches devoted, and the incessant mouthing off of AM sports-radio jocks provided not only a welcome reprieve from the scandalous news of postelection American politics but, all the more, a deserved celebration of the central moment of a great American pastime.

What was unexpected, however, and what should give a modicum of hope to progressives, is that pundits and punters alike sensed a deeper social significance to Super Bowl XXXI. The meeting of the Patriots and the Packers in New Orleans was, in fact, not simply a contest to determine who gets to wear the prized ring, but also a contest between corporate and populist America. Some saw it for what it was, a political drama—a prime-time rematch of traditional midwestern ideals of public ownership against the greed of corporate capital.

A shorter version originally appeared in *The Washington Post* on Super Bowl Sunday, January 26, 1997. Reprinted with permission of the authors.

Following their best season in almost 30 years, the Packers proceeded to win their conference championship by defeating the New South's corporate darling, the Carolina Panthers, and secure the title "America's Team" for the original Titletown USA. That game, played in Lambeau Field on the renowned frozen tundra of northeastern Wisconsin, inspired sportswriters and commentators to recollect the glory days of the Packers—the otherwise defamed 1960s—and to recount tales of the greatest of all football coaches, the late Vince Lombardi, and his unforgettable teams. Anticipating frigid temperatures and snow, sports-channel and network-television stations repeatedly ran videotape of the famous 1967 Ice Bowl in Green Bay between the Packers and the Dallas Cowboys, in which Bart Starr won the game with a quarterback sneak.

Coverage occasionally broke away from gridiron storytelling to consider, in equally nostalgic tones, the city and its irrepressible fans. Standing before tall white snow piles, reporters necessarily referred to Green Bay's legendary winters. They spoke of the citizens' warmth and their ardent loyalty to the Packers through good times and bad, going right back to the beginning more than 76 years ago. Here, it seemed, in this friendly midwestern milltown of 150,000 industrious, tavern-going, working-class men and women (Packer fans come in both sexes), not only professional sports' but also *America*'s finest traditions were alive and well. So much so that in *The Wall Street Journal* the Packers were anointed "the conservative's dream team."

No way. To its credit, the mainstream media noted something that undercut the *Journal*'s all too intuitive linkage of Vince Lombardi's ideological mindset with Green Bay's. Turns out, it is just the opposite; the Packers are the repressed nightmare of the American right. On the Associated Press wire, in the Gannett newspapers, and in *The New York Times* one found stories which suggested that the unique and fundamental feature of the Packers' longevity and, quite possibly, the basis of their success today is that in contrast to every other professional sports franchise, the team is not driven by profits.

The Green Bay Packers are a nonprofit corporation owned by stockholders whose shares yield no dividends, do not grow in value, are not publicly traded, and are widely distributed. Moreover, we all learned that on those several occasions when the organization faced a financial crisis— in the 1920s, 1930s, and 1940s, before pro football was big business—the community readily responded by quickly buying up new stock issues. And— given that Lambeau Field is sold out annually with season ticketholders (who never miss a game) and that there is a 25-year waiting list for those tickets—there is no doubt they would do so again today.

Essentially public property, the Packers have been secured for the generations *and* to the city. Whereas the other small-city founding teams of the

NFL—like Rock Island, Dayton, Marion, Evansville, Akron, and Duluth—folded or moved long ago, the Packers survived and stayed in Green Bay. And every cheesehead knows that, had it been up to the NFL, somewhere along the way the Packers would have been transferred to a bigger city with a larger population and media market. Curiously, if the Packers' board ever did make the unimaginable decision to sell the team, all the monies received—estimated to be up to $150 million—would go to the local Sullivan–Wallen American Legion Post for construction of a war memorial.

It's not only the fans who appreciate the arrangement. As Packer tight-end Keith Jackson put it: "In Green Bay, you're not playing for some owner you don't like." Such words give added meaning to the famous "Lambeau leap"; when a Packer scores a touchdown and jumps into the endzone seats, he's really both demonstrating his affection for the fans and sharing his excitement with the team's owners. (After the NFC championship victory at home, Green Bay fans didn't pour onto the field but warmly welcomed the players into the stands.)

Four days before the Super Bowl on National Public Radio's "Morning Edition," the token leftist guest commentator, Tom Sheibley, a Boston truck-driving member of the Teamsters (with an Amherst B.A. in sociology and Harvard Divinity master's in theology), praised the Packers as an alternative model for today's soulless business culture. Citing the tragedy of Youngstown, Sheibley lamented the corporate lack of civic loyalty and indifference to place, and suggested that locals be allowed to buy and own their corporations as Green Bay folk do the Packers.

Green Bay is a century's-old echo of the midwestern populist tradition with its creed of public ownership. The identification of the city and its team reaches even further back, recalling the ancient Greek city-states, where athletics were part of civic life. On the Monday following their 35–21 triumph in New Orleans, the Packers returned to a parade and stadium reunion for which the entire city turned out as schools, shops, and offices closed. At least 100,000 people young and old lined Green Bay's streets, and an additional 60,000 fans waited six hours in freezing temperatures in Lambeau Field to express their gratitude to coach Mike Holmgren and his players for bringing the Lombardi Trophy back home. A popular T-shirt on sale bore the words "America's Team, The Green Bay Packers—Owned by the People, for the People." Tearful citizens waxed poetic how the snow that fell that day was "confetti from heaven," and there were even reports of "Vince sightings."

Compare this to the New England Patriots, a regional contrivance. Until 1994, the team had never had a season in which it sold out every game. Indeed, who actually knows where Foxboro, Massachusetts, is? But more to the point, the Patriots personify corporate, market-oriented big time sports. Like so many professional teams these days, the Patriots have a history of acquisition and takeover—bouncing from owner to owner, who trade teams as expressions of their own egos and pocketbooks, deserting cities for apparently richer markets or threatening to move in order to compel city governments into building new, publicly financed ballparks. A Patriots' previous owner, Victor Kiam, bought teams as easily as razor companies (Remington). Nor should one forget the Patriots' episode of corporate sleaze: the locker-room harassment in 1990 of sports reporter Lisa Olson. Kiam responded to Olson's lawsuit with a dismissive press conference in which he ridiculed her. (He later apologized and settled out of court.)

The Patriots' present owner, Bob Kraft, seems a cut above his arrogant predecessor with his well-publicized charitable good deeds. But even he, in pursuit of a new stadium, whose construction he says the team will pay for, is demanding free land on the Boston waterfront and placing Boston and Providence in competition for the team.

The Patriots are cursed by corporate hubris. Team members were overshadowed in New Orleans by press stories orchestrated by Parcells's "agent" on their coach's feud with Kraft over who "controlled" the team and whether this was his last game for New England. After the game, all America has witnessed the corporate soap opera of who "owns" Parcells—Bob Kraft and his international paper company or the New York Jets' Leon Hess, board chairman of the Amerada Hess Corporation. The deal was struck. The Hess Corporation gets Parcells, four future draft choices go to the Patriots, and Kraft's charitable foundation gets $300,000. Lost in the moneyed mess was the pathetic news that Parcells didn't even have the decency to return to New England with his team the day after the game. He probably had lawyers to see.

Thirty years ago, Vince Lombardi, who had left the Packers, wanted to return to the NFL to coach the Washington Redskins, though his contract with Green Bay prevented him from coaching elsewhere until 1974. The Packers' board (there never is a Packer "owner") released him and asked no compensation. The board "president" told the press: "I would not cheapen the deal by measuring his worth to us in dollars or a couple of players." Not so Bob Kraft. In corporate sports, draft choices and money are the currency, not class.

There on the sports page, for all to see, played the drama of Super Bowl XXXI. It was not just a confrontation between two outstanding football teams. It was an epic battle between two antithetical ideologies: between a historical, traditional, and besieged one, represented by the Green Bay Packers, in which sports is an organic extension of civic and social life, and a newer, omnipresent one, call it postmodern, represented by the New England Patriots, in which sports, freed from place and loyalty, is merely an extension of the market.

The world champion Green Bay Packers may not actually be "America's team"—in a grand and diverse nation such as ours, who has the right to make such a claim? But they are, in the truest sense, the "people's team" and, thanks to the "fifteen minutes" of media attention afforded to their ownership structure, the Packers might well serve as a model for cities and citizens across the nation as they confront the power and greed of America's corporations.

POSTSCRIPT

In the 1998 National Football League season, the Packers returned to the Super Bowl to face the Denver Broncos. However, this time they lost. In the weeks leading up to Super Bowl Sunday I received a variety of calls from media folk wanting to talk about the town, the fans, and the team. In particular, they asked if the excitement ran as high the second time around in as many years. Of course it did.

At the same time, I followed the press commentary and talked to everyone I could about our prospects (most notably, my friend and dentist, Steve Hein, who happens to serve as the Packers' official team dentist, so, you might say, I regularly get my news straight from the players' mouths). One piece, by conservative columnist Fred Barnes in the *Weekly Standard*, especially annoyed me. Following a visit to Wisconsin to talk to a group of business executives, Barnes wrote "Cheese in My Super Bowl" (January 26, 1998) in which he audaciously claimed that football was a conservative sport, Green Bay a conservative community, and the Packers a conservative team. I replied with the following Letter to the Editor (February 9):

> As a football fan, a resident of Titletown, USA, and an owner of the Green Bay Packers, I take exception to Fred Barnes's portrayal of the sport, our city, and our team as "conservative."
>
> Football a conservative sport? Many of us on the left share Barnes's gridiron passions. And wouldn't Barnes's comrade George Will [conservative commentator *and* author of *Men at Work: The Craft of Baseball* (1990)] resent a love of baseball being construed as a *liberal* affection? Isn't football a leftish game in which a team—of unionized players—collectively struggles to move the ball forward?
>
> Green Bay a conservative city? Admittedly, Joe McCarthy lies buried at the other end of this congressional district, but last year—when the Packers

triumphed in the Super Bowl—Green Bay and northeast Wisconsin chose a Democrat, Jay Johnson, to represent us in Congress, electing him over a conservative Republican.

The Packers a conservative team? Sure, many a prominent player and coach are cultural conservatives, but just as Republicans were able to govern for much of the late 20th century without (until recently) undoing the best of liberalism and social democracy, conservative coaches and players can lead a progressive sports franchise without undoing its truly popular noncapitalist foundations.

More important than the roster is what the Packers, as a community-owned team, represent: an alternative to private ownership. Ask Green Bay's citizens how they would feel about "privatization" of the Packers. Appreciating that corporate priorities remain antagonistic to community and democracy, we know that if our team were fully subordinated to capitalism, we would lose it to some bigger city. Thus, a proto-socialist tradition continues in Green Bay. As one T-shirt declares: "The Green Bay Packers: Owned by the People, for the People."

Sadly, the Packers didn't make it to the Super Bowl this year (1998–99), and worse, our Democratic Congressman ran an abysmal campaign and lost to a conservative Republican in the 1998 elections. But new seasons await.

Chapter 6

FDR: A Great but Flawed President— or Visiting the New Memorial

Arguably, the most important thing to happen in Washington, D.C., this past spring (1997) had little to do with the current crop of Republicans and Democrats and their efforts to reveal each other's campaign-finance shenanigans. What captured popular attention was the long-awaited completion of the Franklin Delano Roosevelt Memorial.

Flying to the nation's capital in late May, I knew I, too, would have to get over to see it. I had in mind recent public-history controversies like the Smithsonian's canceled *Enola Gay* exhibit and the besieged National History Standards, but more than the politics of memory motivated my interest.

Ever since my earliest visit to D.C.—with my Boy Scout troop back in 1961—the city's grand presidential monuments have fascinated me: the gigantic obelisk for George Washington, the "father of his country"; even more so, the Lincoln Memorial, with Abe himself sitting majestically within, his eyes gazing out on the Mall—sometimes upon citizens mobilized in protest of persistent injustices; and, especially, the column-encircled and rotunda-capped Jefferson Memorial (dedicated by FDR himself in 1943), wherein stands the radical patriot and author of the Declaration of Independence.

A stop at the new Roosevelt Memorial seemed all the more appropriate since I had traveled to Washington for an organizing meeting of Scholars, Artists, and Writers for Social Justice (SAWSJ). Looking to the future, we envisioned creating a network of pro–labor movement intellectuals. But we all knew our efforts also recalled the 1930s alliance of insurgent industrial workers and progressive "cultural workers" (see Chapter 7).

I needed to see if the new memorial did more than celebrate FDR's accomplishments in confronting the Depression and the Second World War. In this supposedly post-heroic age, I even wondered if it invited us to consider Roosevelt's mistakes and failures.

Originally appeared in *The Times Higher Education Supplement*, August 29, 1997.

I had read the political right's critiques. Though various conservatives offered (cynical) praise of Roosevelt, the monument's unveiling led a few reactionaries to restate their perverse historical understandings and sympathies. Pat Buchanan accused Roosevelt of "lying" about keeping America out of World War II and of "appeasing" Stalin. Even more outrageously, Joseph Sobran charged FDR with "abolishing constitutional government" and—as if such comparisons are worthwhile—of forming an "alliance with a worse tyrant than Hitler, Mussolini, or Hirohito." No doubt, Buchanan and Sobran also find fault with Roosevelt's remark that "if American democracy ceases to move forward as a living force, seeking day and night by peaceful means to better the lot of our citizens, fascism will grow in strength in our land."

Of course, I had radically different concerns. Mine had to do with Roosevelt's inadequate response to the plight of Europe's Jews and his Executive Order placing Japanese Americans in concentration camps for the duration of the war. Strangely enough, I actually found the words of conservative columnist Ralph de Toledano helpful here: "Franklin Delano Roosevelt was a great president—and he well merits the monument.... But to subscribe to that honor does not oblige us to ignore that perfection exists in no man. Moses was not allowed to enter the Promised Land because he had transgressed. FDR was a great president, but like all great men his flaws, too, were great."

In any case, given the *un*likelihood that the FDR Memorial treated those subjects, I hoped that it at least asked us to reflect on the thirty-second president's unfulfilled aspirations, particularly his 1944 call to extend the Constitution's Bill of Rights, that is, to create an "Economic Bill of Rights." In this vein, I had found the Memorial's dedication ceremonies utterly offensive. Less than a year earlier, Bill Clinton and the Republican-dominated Congress had gotten together to trash Roosevelt's legacy by passing a so-called Welfare Reform Act ending the federal government's guarantee of support to the poor. Now, these very same folks had the gall to reunite and dedicate the monument to Roosevelt's memory!

Accompanied by my sister and her three-year-old son, who live in Washington, I ventured over to the Memorial on a bright, warm, and humid morning. Roosevelt himself had once said that if he were ever to be accorded a monument, he would like merely that a stone be placed in front of the National Archives bearing the words "In memory of . . . " However, designed by Lawrence Halprin, the Memorial is the first presidential monument in the form of an entire landscape.[1]

The Memorial is situated on a seven-and-a-half acre strip of land between the Tidal Basin and the Potomac River. It is constructed of 4000 South Dakota red-granite blocks and composed of four sequential open-air rooms adorned with waterfalls, pools, sculptures, and inscriptions of selected quotes from Roosevelt's speeches. The Memorial is vast; indeed, it's actually more like a park than a monument. *Progressive* writer Ruth Coniff went so far as to refer to it as a "theme park."

Prior to the Memorial's dedication, the hot media issue had been whether or not Roosevelt, who had suffered from polio, should be depicted in his wheelchair (which he himself had studiously avoided using when appearing publicly before journalists' cameras). Halprin had decided against posing FDR in the wheelchair; yet, as Halprin reminded everyone, he had designed the Memorial back in 1974 and, though no requirement existed to do so at the time, he had fashioned it to be fully accessible to the disabled.

All history and politics aside, my young nephew loved it. He could not resist the opportunity to run, climb, clamber, and, if he had had his way, soak himself in the pools. I wish I could have joined him, but I was trying to make sense of it all.

I am still not really sure what I think of the Memorial. The four main rooms render a narrative of Roosevelt's four terms (1933–45): the Depression, the New Deal, World War II, and the postwar challenges that his death kept him from facing. The location, the scale, the formation, the stonework, the falls, make it truly magnificent. The sculptures of an Appalachian farm couple, Depression-era breadline, and Fireside Chat radio listener by George Segal, along with the works and carvings by other artists treating FDR's New Deal and wartime initiatives, and Neil Ersten's statues of First Lady Eleanor Roosevelt and Franklin Roosevelt seated with his Scottish terrier, Fala, effectively evoke the past. And yet, with homeless Americans living rough, only blocks away, there's something perverse about folks positioning themselves "on the breadline" to have photos taken.

In its favor, the Memorial does end up recounting more than the political achievements of a remarkable figure. It offers a political testament to present and future generations. Though the envisioned Economic Bill of Rights is nowhere cited, engraved on the granite wall of the last room are the "Four Freedoms" pronounced by Roosevelt in his annual message to Congress of January 1941: "FREEDOM OF SPEECH—FREEDOM OF WORSHIP—FREEDOM FROM WANT—FREEDOM FROM FEAR."[2] One can only hope that they challenge visitors.

Moreover, in this age of triumphant capital, corporate hegemony, and conservative politics, the Memorial's historical references also testify to the contradictions of capitalism, the depredations of an unregulated market, *and* the possibility of addressing them through public and social-democratic action.

Chapter 7

LABOR AND THE INTELLECTUALS: A NEW CULTURAL FRONT?

After a generation of defeat and retreat, American labor has started to fight back and, once again, aspires to be a powerful force for social change. Remembering a time when industrial workers and cultural workers marched together, labor's leadership has invited intellectuals, artists, and students to join in the redemption and reinvigoration of America's progressive tradition. And, excited by labor's call, we have begun to mobilize.

Twenty-five years ago, American capital reneged on its postwar "social contract" with organized labor—the unions of the American Federation of Labor and Congress of Industrial Organizations (AFL-CIO)—to pursue a class war from above. In favor of increased profits and greater management control, corporate bosses sought to roll back workers' wages and benefits and, if possible, to "bust" their unions.

Bankrolling the ascendance of the New Right and Reaganism, business has succeeded in advancing its cause on all fronts. Unprepared to respond to the offensive, the organized share of the labor force has fallen back from 25 percent to 14 percent. Today, capital rules and, while the rich have grown richer, working folk have grown poorer.

Down but not out, in October 1995 the AFL-CIO unions elected John Sweeney and his "new voice" team to lead them. Sweeney promised a fresh commitment to "organizing the unorganized," addressing the needs of women and minorities, and promoting the interests of all working people. In speeches and a book, *America Needs a Raise*,[1] Sweeney spoke of seeking allies for labor and of placing labor at the heart of a new progressive movement. He publicly positioned himself on the left—and provocatively distinguished himself from his predecessors—by joining Democratic Socialists of America.

Originally appeared in *The Times Higher Education Supplement*, October 3, 1997.

Sweeney and his lieutenants quickly moved to restructure AFL-CIO operations. They gave top priority to organizing and began to try out new ideas, like "Union Summer 1996." Modeled after Freedom Summer, the 1964 civil rights drive, Union Summer successfully recruited almost 1500 college students to serve in community and workplace organizing efforts around the country. In 1997, they added "Senior Summer" in which retirees enlisted to work alongside the younger recruits.

Inspired by labor's actions, Steve Fraser, a New York book editor and historical writer, and Nelson Lichtenstein, a University of Virginia history professor, organized a fall 1996 "Teach-In with the Labor Movement" (fashioned after the Vietnam teach-ins of the sixties). In addition to John Sweeney, a host of literary and scholarly celebrities—including Betty Friedan, Eric Foner, David Montgomery, Frances Fox Piven, Norman Birnbaum, Cornell West, and Richard Rorty—addressed an overflow crowd of 2500 at Columbia University in New York City.

Opinions at the teach-in diverged on several matters, particularly on questions of the relations between labor and race, gender and "identity politics."[2] Nevertheless, every speaker welcomed labor's new militancy and progressivism, and each reiterated the call for an alliance of unionists and intellectuals. No doubt, all of them had in mind both the 1930s, when intellectuals rallied to the cause of the labor movement, and the 1960s, when, sadly, divisions over the Vietnam War deeply alienated the academic left and students from organized labor.[3]

Those of us who have sought to serve as *democratic* public intellectuals—and break out of the trap critically described by Russell Jacoby exactly ten years ago in *The Last Intellectuals*[4]—have come to realize that we need to reconnect with the union movement. We appreciate the intimate connection between the class war against labor and the concurrent culture war against academic humanists. Moreover, we ourselves have witnessed the increasing subordination of our own "trades" to the imperatives of capital, entailing budget cuts, downsizing, and the spread of part-time labor.

Liberal and left periodicals like *Dissent, Lingua Franca, DoubleTake, Boston Review, Monthly Review, The Baffler, Bad Subjects, Mother Jones, New Politics, Social Text, Tikkun*, and *The Nation* have taken up the "labor question" in a big way in 1997. Editors have devoted entire issues to work, the working class, and the new labor movement. In fact, the publisher M. E. Sharpe has launched a new bimonthly magazine, *Working USA*.

Other signs of a new national sentiment sympathetic to labor have appeared. The popular photo magazine, *Life*, has issued a special spring edition dedicated to "Celebrating Our Heroes," which includes *labor* organizers and activists like Mother Jones and Cesar Chavez in its pantheon.

Here, in Wisconsin, the state legislature has come close to passing a bill that would require schools to teach the history of the labor movement. The popular nightly television quiz show, *Wheel of Fortune*, recently saluted "Working Families and their Unions" with a week of "union-member only" contestants. And, most notably, a strike and victory at the giant United Parcel Service by the (hitherto scorned) Teamsters Union received widespread popular support.

Yet perhaps the renewed attention accorded to the labor movement by its enemies testifies best to the changes taking place in the unions. Rightwing columnists have returned to bitterly attacking labor's new leadership. Union-busting law firms once again have started to aggressively advertise their skills. And the conservative think-tank, the American Enterprise Institute, has published Max Green's *Epitaph for American Labor*, which closes with a warning about the new *rapprochement* between labor and the intellectual left.[5] Presumably, conservatives worry that their vaunted "end of history" has itself begun to come to an end.

Indeed, a movement might actually be in the making. The Columbia teach-in instigated 20 other similar events across the nation, and colleagues have scheduled more for the coming semesters.

Thrilled by developments, the organizers of the first teach-in called together sixty of us—known for our pro-labor writings and activities—in hopes of forming a national network of intellectuals and artists in support of the "new" labor movement. Meeting in late May at American University in Washington, D.C., participants ranged in age from veterans of the postwar progressive campaigns, to those of us from the 1960s (the majority present), to several "twenty-somethings" involved in graduate student organizing or off-campus labor initiatives.

Energy and enthusiasm filled the room. Truly, I could not recall a more hopeful assemblage of left intellectuals. Both John Sweeney and the AFL-CIO's new executive vice-president, Linda Chavez-Thompson, spoke to the group. Our eagerness to work with them clearly delighted them and, so inclined, we spent the greater part of the meeting discussing our prospects and possible projects.

At the end of the day, tired but united, we resolved to create a new organization. Twenty of us met as a steering committee during the summer via e-mail, and a couple of times in New York, to work out the basic details. Finally, on September 1, 1997—America's Labor Day—we launched "Scholars, Artists, and Writers for Social Justice."

We've received a tremendous response from within and without the academy. In the months ahead, we plan to convene a national meeting, likely dedicated to "The Rights of Workers," and, in tandem with labor unions and other progressive groups, we envision formulating an Economic

Bill of Rights. Together, workers and intellectuals might yet make history anew, audaciously and democratically.

POSTSCRIPT

Scholars, Artists, and Writers for Social Justice (SAWSJ) survives. But its future remains problematic. Indeed, at times it seemed SAWSJ would never even get off the ground. (In 1997–98, I served on both the organization's National Steering Committee and its smaller executive Coordinating Committee.) We discovered we did not all agree about organizational structure, relations with the AFL-CIO, or the projects and events we hoped to realize. We never fully resolved those issues, but, fortunately, our shared aspirations to join with labor in pursuit of democratic social change transcended our respective notions of what the organization should look like.

The central question of organizational structure dealt with whether SAWSJ should primarily develop as a national network of individual intellectuals or as a network of "locals." While debate ensued, SAWSJ developed organically. Individuals joined, but in places where local chapters could form—such as in the larger cities and/or on campuses where numbers permit—they did so, and they have coordinated their activities with other local progressive groups.

The big question regarding SAWSJ's relations with the AFL-CIO had to do with just how closely we should align ourselves with the Federation. Reservations about getting too intimate originated in doubts about the new leadership's commitment to organizing the unorganized and challenging the power of capital, and about just how deeply down the changes at the top actually reached.

In any case, good relations with the AFL-CIO were essential in securing needed resources for and assistance in staging major events and enhancing SAWSJ's visibility. Still, reservations have persisted. Leaders can be changed or stymied in their efforts. For example, the election of Jimmy Hoffa, Jr., to head the Teamsters in the wake of fresh scandals (following, ironically, the union's marvelous triumph in the UPS strike) gave SAWSJ members good reason to feel anxious about the prospects of progressive labor. Moreover, some of us believed the AFL-CIO should be even more generous than it has been in support of SAWSJ's plans and labors. We also worried about how we might engage the National Education Association in our efforts.

Yet another question we grappled with had to do with the kinds of events and campaigns the organization should mount. Some argued in favor of high-profile, celebrity-filled media events in order to make as big a public impact as possible, and others have urged more grassroots initiatives in order to build the organization's base. Though I might originally have favored the latter, I strenuously pushed for the former, in light of the success and reverberations of the Columbia teach-in. I did so, in particular, because SAWSJ seemed a predominantly "coastal" affair, especially East Coast. To more effectively reach the American heartland, I felt we had to get media coverage and/or attention, for example, on C-SPAN. In the end, we found ways to compromise.

On a weekend in late spring 1998, we held our first major SAWSJ event—"Democracy and the Labor Movement"—in Washington, D.C., on the campus of George Washington University. Drawing more than 500 people, we kicked off on the Friday evening with a panel of speakers hosted by civil rights veteran Julian Bond and composed of both renowned intellectuals (but not jet-setters) and front-line union activists, plus AFL-CIO President John Sweeney. For the Saturday, we arranged a wide variety of sessions on the conference theme, intended for academics and activists alike. And on Sunday morning, SAWSJ members convened to create an official structure and elect new leadership. (At that time, many of us who first founded the organization stepped aside in favor of new folk and fresh energies.)

In 1998–99, the leadership of SAWSJ resolved to hold the next national meeting at Yale University in order to call attention to graduate student and university service workers' organizing drives nationally, and the ongoing campaigns at Yale in particular. This fit well with the AFL-CIO's declared national campaign for workers' "right to organize." (Also, during that year SAWSJ established national offices at the University of Massachusetts in the Labor Education and Research Center.)

In April 1999, more than 600 SAWSJ members and sympathizers gathered in New Haven under the banner "Challenging Corporate Control." Once again, the event opened with speeches by leading labor and intellectual personages, proceeded with sessions wherein scholars and activists exchanged ideas, and closed with a "business" session to select leaders and decide upon an agenda for the coming year. Members formally committed SAWSJ to the AFL-CIO's "Right to Organize" campaign, formulated plans for an op-ed writing network, and—recognizing the growth of students activism, especially regarding labor issues—resolved that SAWSJ should reach out to interested undergraduates to encourage their activities and recruit them into the labor movement.

Labor's struggles continue, and growing numbers of academics and students seek to make contributions. Furthermore, as organized labor defines its struggle in terms of workers' rights as citizens, and reaches out to groups too long ignored or alienated, civil rights groups have begun to shift their attentions from social to economic issues. (In that spirit the editors of *Sojourners* magazine produced a special September 1998 issue, "Good Works: Why the Church Needs the Labor Movement, and Vice Versa.")

Finally, we should note Daniel Nelson's article "What Happened to Organized Labor?" After so many writings already had appeared on the subject, its publication in July 1999 should have come as no surprise. However, it was notable not only because it offered a sympathetic historical analysis of labor's woes and a relatively optimistic view of its prospects but also because it appeared in a conservative magazine, the Forbes-owned *American Heritage*.[6]

SAWSJ itself may not survive or succeed, but I think we will have encouraged greater numbers of academics and students to stand in solidarity with labor than would have had we failed to respond to labor's invitation.

Chapter 8

UP-ENDING THE END OF HISTORY, REDEEMING AMERICA'S PROPHETIC MEMORY

History does not speak for itself. Our antagonists have long comprehended this. They have understood that the liberation of capital and the making of a new corporate order require reshaping historical memory, consciousness, and imagination. Their very name—conservatives—registers their proprietary interest in the past.

Indeed, however much conservatives claim to venerate America's heritage while truly dreading it, pretend to defend American history while really seeking to suppress it, and pose as champions of American traditions while actually advocating policies that corrupt them, they do seem to value the powers of the past more than we do on the democratic left, and they've been wielding them more aggressively than we have.

Naturally, we must reject their practices and contest their pronouncements. At the same time, we should not fail to look into their politics of history and try to appreciate what motivates it—we may even find it empowering.

From the time of the New Right's formation more than 20 years ago, through its continuing battles against working people, minorities, and the left, conservative politics clearly has been marked by persistent appeals to "history."

The very fashioning of the New Right coalition entailed the fabrication of a "past" capable of attracting such diverse folks as the corporate elite, free marketeers, moral majoritarians, cold warriors, and a host of traditional, neo-, and paleo-conservatives. Their respective ideals and enemies were (and still are) varied and, even, contradictory. Yet—in the wake of the progressive 1960s, in the midst of the crises of the 1970s, and in the face

---

Originally appeared in *Review of Education, Pedagogy and Cultural Studies*, vol. 20, no. 4, December 1998. This chapter originated as a talk presented at the Center for Democratic Values conference—"Arguing with the Right"—held in Columbus, Ohio, in November 1997.

of a then still-imaginable broad-left coalition—the Reagan Republicans' use and abuse of history drew them close enough together to make a movement of them.

Reagan himself harkened back nostalgically to some time before the Great Society of the 1960s or the New Deal of the 1930s, depending upon the audience and the occasion. He conjured up a "lost America": a "stand tall" America unilaterally prepared to assert its interests abroad; a virtuous America peopled by God-fearing, hard-working, self-sufficient families and respectful, well-educated, school-praying children; an America uncorrupted by foreign policy syndromes, welfare programs, workplace regulations, environmental restrictions, educational reforms, affirmative action, and women's rights.

Envisioning a "new morning" for the nation, Reagan promised a politics of restoration. He did not find fault with America or Americans—at least, not all Americans. He targeted liberals, leftists, feminists, trade unionists, welfare recipients, minorities, and university intellectuals.

"The past" remained central to Reagan and his comrades' rhetoric following their 1980 election triumph. History framed Reagan's every speech, and historical references adorned his every line. Not just in the predictable manner. Knowing that the American Revolution continued to inspire, Reagan mobilized its memory. Outrageously, he resurrected the Founding Fathers in defense of his administration's acts of state terrorism in Central America.

Knowing that the majority of Americans still identified themselves as Democrats and remained committed to FDR's New Deal legacy and, even, to LBJ's Great Society initiatives, the Reaganites audaciously recruited dead liberals and progressives to their cause. Reagan himself quoted Franklin Roosevelt—completely out of context—to attack welfare and welfare recipients; and he and his cabinet cronies regularly cited the Reverend Martin Luther King's anti-racialist aspirations as posthumous blessings of their crusades against affirmative action.

It was always more than a matter of enhancing Republican policy initiatives. New Rightists set out to undo what remained of the liberal consensus and postwar social contract in favor of establishing a new conservative regime and corporate hegemony. They longed to declare the capitalist order eternal, and—given the ongoing disintegration of the Soviet Empire—they could not contain themselves. Handsomely supported by the Olin Foundation, in 1989 Francis Fukuyama fulfilled every ruling class's fantasy by proclaiming "The End of History."

No fools, conservatives knew that securing political hegemony entailed more than monopolizing political discourse—they knew it took even more than the implosion of Soviet Communism. They knew it involved rearticulating the grand narrative of American and world history and construing contemporary events and developments in those terms. Hoping to convince Americans that the way things are is the way they *ought* to be, conservatives knew they had to advance a governing narrative that would celebrate the present order of things as the culmination and universal fulfillment of history. Their efforts to formulate and propagate such a narrative commenced well before Fukuyama gave away their ambitions.

Conservatives anxiously appreciated the work of the new radical historians who, inspired by the movements of the sixties, had begun to reclaim history from the bottom up. Such work recovered the struggles from below that had made America freer, more egalitarian and democratic—and demonstrated that the movements of the sixties themselves stood firmly in their tradition.

Recognizing the threat, the right resolved to prevent the new history's influence from spreading. Think back: Before anyone claimed that Johnny and Jane couldn't read and write—before anyone lamented the loss of the literary canon or decried "political correctness"—conservatives protested that Johnny and Jane were dangerously ignorant of history and launched the culture wars by turning this "crisis of historical education" into an issue of national security and cohesiveness.

New Right politicians and pundits didn't just demand the teaching of *more* history; they demanded the teaching of a more *conservative* history. Taking aim at the new generation of critical scholars and teachers, they insisted that historians and their humanities colleagues were to blame for the crisis. From their bully pulpits at the Department of Education and National Endowment for the Humanities, William Bennett and Lynne Cheney accused us of painting a monochromatically dark picture of America's past, "teaching ideology," and subverting the nation's culture and "shared values."

Purges were out, so they resorted to issuing recommended course syllabi and calling for the enactment of government-sponsored and -endorsed "national standards for history." Their broadsides and pamphlets testified to their ambitions to transmit officially sanctioned curricula that neglected not only American and Western exploitation and oppression but also our histories of popular resistance, rebellion, and revolution.

In 1991, Cheney commissioned the writing of national standards, fully expecting she would be in a position to approve the product and oversee its implementation. But, of course, in 1992 Clinton beat Bush; Cheney took refuge at the American Enterprise Institute; and the authors of the national standards for history were no longer subject to the right's immediate supervision.

Ironically, the standards—which appeared two years later after a long, professional, and thorough review process—reflected the very knowledge and questions the conservatives so despised and had been so eager to keep out of classrooms.

Though no longer possessed of official posts and titles, the right did not retreat. In fact, its rhetoric became all the more strident and virulent. Powerless to manage the process by which the national standards for history had been composed, conservatives orchestrated a campaign—from AM talk-radio shows to the floors of Congress—that portrayed the standards as anti-American and its authors as traitors. The 1994 election results placed the national standards for history in political and educational limbo.

In a similar fashion, conservatives attacked a series of public history exhibits in Washington. Most notably, they forced the Smithsonian to scrap plans for a National Air and Space Museum display on the 50th anniversary of the dropping of the atomic bomb on Japan because, instead of simply commemorating the event, curators had planned to pose historical questions about it.

After two decades, the right continues to dominate the nation's political discourse, capital seems to rule more confidently than ever, and we live the consequences of their class war from above.

True—the right has failed to dictate an official history to be transmitted by our schools. True—it has failed to promulgate a grand governing narrative, which celebrates the present order of things as the universal fulfillment of history. And true—it has failed to persuade Americans that the way things are is the way they ought to be (probably an impossible task to begin with, given a polity originally constituted by revolutionaries, a culture regularly refreshed by the children of slaves, peasants, artisans, and industrial workers, and a society inevitably riven by class inequality and conflict).

Nevertheless, the right apparently has succeeded in propagating an understanding of present and future possibilities that favors corporate hegemony and conservative governance. To most Americans, while things are not the way they ought to be, they seem the only way they can be. We have been depoliticized. We stare at the end of history.

Yet even as I say that, I know the dialectic which is history also continues to express itself, and once again—perhaps more than ever in a generation—real possibilities for radical- and social-democratic politics and ideas are presenting themselves and demanding our attention and agency.

If the right's periodicals are to be believed, conservatives themselves are falling further and further into disarray as their inherent divisions reassert themselves.

Even more crucially, the election of John Sweeney's "New Voice" team to leadership of the AFL-CIO has reinvigorated labor and class politics.

Promising to restore *movement* to the labor movement, Sweeney and his lieutenants have recommitted the Federation to organizing the unorganized and to serving the interests of all working people, men and women, in all their diversity. Looking for friends, they have begun to reach out to other groups and organizations. And, recalling the 1930s alliances of industrial and cultural workers, they have called for unionists and left intellectuals to repair the breach that opened wide between us in the 1960s. In response, we find our students signing up for "Union Summers" and ourselves participating in "Labor Teach-Ins" and new pro-labor organizations such as Scholars, Artists, and Writers for Social Justice.

Of course, nothing is inevitable; there are no assurances that we will get it together; there are no guarantees that, if we do, we will prevail. Still, there is good reason to hope *and* to act.

Taking seriously our antagonists' original and persistent anxieties and worries, we might start by asking: What has motivated their unrelenting desire to control the past? What drives their incessant corruptions, suppressions, and fabrications of history?

The answer: Conservatives fear America's "prophetic memory." They well know that the making of America—with all its exploitation and oppression—has been a process of democratic struggle. And they well know how that continuous struggle—with all its tragedies and ironies—has entailed victories and proffered possibilities for the future. Thus, they rightly fear history and necessarily try to control it, for it attests that we most definitely can secure greater freedom, equality, and democracy.

So, what is to be done? I repeat my opening words: History does not speak for itself. If we really do aspire to make history and create a freer, more equal and democratic America, now and in the future, then—among other things—we will have to make far more of *the past* than we have been making. At the least, we will have to do so in a way different than we have been doing.

We have spent years criticizing and deconstructing American life; but we have failed to reconstruct and promote a vision of what America might yet become *and* how we might achieve it. Instead of fomenting hope and a sense of possibility, we too often have ended up merely contributing to despair and cynicism and bolstering the illusion that the way things are is the only way they can be.

We fail ourselves and we fail our fellow citizens if by our intellectual labors we merely reinforce pessimism and resignation. We must not, we should not, *and* we need not do so.

We have got to evoke and advance the exceptional narrative of our nation's diverse democratic struggles. And we must reveal the triumphs and, yes, the *progress* accomplished by our predecessors and ourselves.

Moreover, we need to imbue contemporary historical memory, consciousness, and imagination with the aspirations and visions of those who struggled before us and for us.

We must not mimic the right. Hell, we don't need to. A generation of scholarly labors affords us a wealth of history to draw upon in favor of cultivating a progressive and inviting grand narrative of American experience and possibilities. Remember the accomplishments we have to build upon: We won a revolutionary war for independence, we abolished slavery, we enacted universal suffrage, we established labor's right to organize, we secured civil rights for minorities . . .

Recall the radicals who have empowered us to do so. I cite only a few: Tom Paine, Sojourner Truth, Frederick Douglass, Walt Whitman, Eugene Debs, Mother Jones, John Reed, Dorothy Day, Woody Guthrie, Paul Robeson, I. F. Stone, Ella Josephine Baker, Martin Luther King, Michael Harrington, Cesar Chavez.

To up-end the end of history, we have got to redeem America's *prophetic memory*.[1]

Chapter 9

GETTING BACK OUR BITE

A couple of years ago, an editor at the *Green Bay Press Gazette* asked me if I would read Marvin Cetron and Owen Davies's *Probable Futures: How Science and Technology Will Transform Our Lives in the Next Twenty Years*.[1] He wanted to talk about the "next century" with the intention of publishing our exchange in the paper. Always anxious to reach new audiences, I accepted the invitation.

Co-authored by a corporate consultant and a science writer, the book celebrated our extraordinary prospects yet made no reference to power, property, and wealth. When I reported back to the editor, insisting that we ourselves should also address political *and* democratic possibilities, he quickly lost interest in having the conversation. It angered me, but I understood. The book's "utopianism" rendered no serious challenge and, likely, the editor had wanted to write an entertaining, *not* a critical, piece.

Last year, a socialist magazine asked me to review Roberto Unger and Cornel West's *The Future of American Progressivism: An Initiative for Political and Economic Reform*.[2] Given the authors' prominence, and the way their book was being touted, I eagerly read it in search of fresh ideas and inspiration. But it lacked both. Though Unger and West recognized the challenges, they deferred to the triumph of the market and merely proposed a fancy mix of policy proposals and theological niceties. Terribly disappointed, and with little good to say, I killed the review myself.

Comprehending American history as a struggle to shape the nation's inherent revolutionary and utopian impulses, we would have to say the contest seems to have become decidedly one-sided. Arguably, the Disney Corporation and its "imagineers" now represent our utopian vanguard. What has happened to the left's imagination and vision?

Russell Jacoby wonders the same in *The End of Utopia: Politics and Culture in an Age of Apathy*.[3] He observes that politics has become boring, but not necessarily benign, and that our future is reduced to a choice between

---

Originally appeared in a somewhat shorter version in *The Progressive*, September 1999.

"the status quo or something worse." He agonizes that a "utopian spirit—a sense that the future could transcend the present—has vanished." And he holds his comrades on the left accountable: "Radicals have lost their bite, liberals their backbone."

In the face of recent history, Jacoby grants that retreating to rethink ideas and strategies would have been understandable and, even, honorable. But instead the left's withdrawal has entailed accepting the priorities of the powers that be and/or subscribing to causes that, however admirable, represent little more than tinkering with the present system. Worse still, too many leftists have had the audacity to pretend that "every step backward or sideways marks ten steps forward."

Jacoby chastises the left for deferring and, all the more, for dissembling. His several chapters survey radicalism's evacuation and liberalism's emptiness, the reduction of progressivism to multiculturalism, the supercession of democratic cultural criticism by populist cultural studies, the institutionalization of intellectual life, the abandonment of universalism in favor of particularism, and the neutering of utopianism.

Jacoby compares the 1990s to the 1950s. In the fifties, pundits pronounced the "end of ideology." Yet events of the sixties proved dramatically otherwise. Or did they? In 1989, Francis Fukuyama declared the "end of history," and so far it seems he ain't wrong. Radicals, liberals, even many socialists, now recite the verities of the market, assuming there is "no alternative." Ironically, we hear the greatest reservations from conservatives like John Gray in *False Dawn* and financiers like George Soros in *The Crisis of Global Capitalism*.[4] Still, nobody speaks of a life beyond capitalism.

Lacking alternatives, leftists ardently promote the cause of diversity and multiculturalism. Here, too, Jacoby recalls the 1950s. Asserting that multiculturalism simply repackages pluralism, though admittedly with an ethnic twist, he reminds us that cold warriors posed American pluralism against foreign "totalitarianism" and continually used the latter concept, originally crafted to refer to both Fascism and Communism, to broadly damn the politics of the left, in particular.

Jacoby appreciates multiculturalism's humanism and the need for ethnic and gender representation in offices and texts; however, he maintains that "no vision drives multiculturalism" other than, perhaps, "inclusiveness"—and that implies conformity. Pluralism/multiculturalism, he charges, is the "opium of disillusioned intellectuals."

Is America actually a multicultural society? Noting the increasingly indiscriminate application of the term "culture," Jacoby points out that "identity" does not necessarily equal "culture"; multiplying identities do not themselves make America a *multicultural* society; and, in fact, "the melting pot did happen—and is happening." He repeats that we should welcome scholarly and pedagogical interest in the diversity of American experience. But, he warns, we should neither reify such diversity nor exaggerate the subversiveness of multiculturalist ideology.

Jacoby proceeds to deconstruct academic cultural studies. For all their radical posturing, he says, cultural-studies scholars end up merely celebrating the status quo. Not only does their postmodern rhetoric alienate them from the very people in whose lives they profess a concern, but also their populist desires lead them to uncritically embrace "mass culture" and, thus, to overlook the difference between the former and *democratic* culture.

Postulating that the fate of utopian vision is tied to the fate of intellectuals—leftist intellectuals—Jacoby explains why we're in serious trouble. Intellectuals "have migrated into institutions to become specialists and professionals. At the same time, they have turned suspicious of universal categories as unscientific or oppressive." He cannot resist mocking various figures of the intellectual-academic elite for bemoaning their supposedly marginal status even as they pursue lives of privilege and renown.

Most troubling, Jacoby states, intellectuals have abandoned universalism in favor of localisms and particularisms. Denying the possibility of objectivity and truth, they aestheticize reality, repudiate the liberating promise of Enlightenment universals, and seem incapable of making firm moral judgments. In essence, they take cultural relativism to the extreme and never get to the fundamental political issue: "What is, and what should be?"

Finally, Jacoby notes that at the end of the twentieth century dread has overwhelmed desire, *anti*-utopianism has overpowered utopianism. Aside from the "futurists," who cheerfully acclaim liberation through science, technology, and cyberspace ("the utopians of an anti-utopian age"), who dares to envision and propose a future different from and preferable to the present?

Though Jacoby realizes history has not come to a close and expects the utopian spirit to some day reassert itself, if and when it does, it will be no thanks to our contemporary intellectual cohorts.

Does Russell Jacoby beating up on the intellectual left seem familiar? It should, for it's the third time in a dozen years he has done so. In *The Last Intellectuals*,[5] he recounted how the radicals of the 1960s had turned into the professors of the 1980s, conquering academe but, at the same time, enclosing themselves within its walls and abdicating politics and public life to the right. And in *Dogmatic Wisdom*,[6] even as he revealed the culture wars as essentially a sham campaign by the right to deflect attention from the critical issues confronting Americans, he accused leftist academics of failing to engage their fellow citizens on those issues *and* of exploiting the culture wars to enhance their own positions.

I praised those books. However much Jacoby underestimated the right's capacity to contain the left within higher education, conflated postmodernists with the left as a whole, and ignored other progressive currents, he diagnosed the left's spreading afflictions, like inane writing, excessive theorizing, and self-promotion (otherwise known as the "French flu").

Don't get me wrong. I also enjoyed *The End of Utopia*. Jacoby's arguments, especially regarding multiculturalism and cultural studies, bear repeating. Furthermore, Jacoby continues to demonstrate his brilliance as an intellectual historian. For example, in order to prove that democratic cultural criticism does not mean refusing to make qualitative distinctions, he rescues Matthew Arnold, the English writer, from the evil clutches of conservatives (whose claims to Arnold leftists have rarely contested). He shows how Arnold defended "high culture" not for elites and upper classes, but for all citizens, and proffered a firmly democratic and egalitarian critique of Victorian culture and society by articulating how class inequalities and market priorities impoverish all aspects of life. In contrast to that of cultural-studies folk, Arnold's approach challenges the existing social order by envisioning a richer, more egalitarian, and more democratic life than that afforded by capitalism.

Nevertheless, Jacoby's denunciations do grow wearisome and are, quite frankly, no longer so original. Among others, Todd Gitlin has written on the postmodernist left's foolish abandonment of universalism in *The Twilight of Common Dreams*, and Richard Rorty has echoed Jacoby's own frustrations about the academic left's failure to serve as a class of public intellectuals in *Achieving Our Country*.[7]

Jacoby closes by asking "What is to be done?" Yet, oddly enough, having written of utopian thinking, he offers no more hope than to wait and see what history brings. From Jacoby's own chapters, we can derive a model of democratic criticism. But, after all his attacks, he owes us more. His crankiness, and sense of estrangement from the left, seem to get in his way.

Jacoby might have considered America's radical tradition and utopian impulse, and how we might yet redeem and renew them. He, at least, should have attended to the work of his comrades who have not drowned themselves in postmodernism. He ignores too many of us. And thus he remains oblivious to potentially significant progressive developments and possibilities.

Marx and Engels criticized utopian socialists for assuming that praiseworthy beliefs and ideas alone are sufficient to transform society. Ideas, they knew, must engage movement and struggle. Jacoby has written smart criticism and good history, but he has yet to radically connect.

Chapter 10

1968–1998

May usually brings thoughts of the summer ahead. This year it brought thoughts of 30 years ago. I had planned at semester's end to throw myself into nineteenth-century American history. However, even before I had my students' papers graded, two new books—*1968: Magnum Throughout the World*, a collection of photographs introduced by Eric Hobsbawm and Marc Weitzmann, and *1968: Marching in the Streets*, a well-illustrated narrative by Tariq Ali and Susan Watkins—stole my attention and took me back three decades.[1]

I read slowly through the two volumes. I paused at certain pages to savor the radical-democratic dreams and possibilities that their images and words evoked, at others to grasp the truly global character of the year's risings and repressions, and at yet others to avoid having to confront anew the ensuing tragedies and disappointments.

I could not keep the reading and remembering to myself. At lunch, I asked my colleagues for their reminiscences of 1968. They had reactions of a similar sort. They started by referring to where they each had been—from grad school in Madison, Wisconsin, to fieldwork in southern Italy—and proceeded, in a joking manner, to recount some very personal, ahistorical kinds of experiences, as if trying to evade reference to the public events of that year.

Yet, when pressed, they spoke of Vietnam and anti-war marches, political campaigns and assassinations, Yippies and Chicago "police riots," Prague Spring and Soviet occupation, May '68 in Paris, "Black Power" and Black Panthers, the Mexico City Olympics and the Mexican government's suppression of popular protests . . .

Magazine articles—the best, Christopher Hitchens's "The Children of '68" in the June 1998 issue of *Vanity Fair* [2]—and retrospectives by the BBC World Service and National Public Radio further propelled my anamnesis. On reflection, all my memories seemed those of a spectator and, with

---

Originally appeared in *The Times Higher Education Supplement*, July 3, 1998.

much more reason to feel regretful than Hitchens, I found myself repeating his words about "not having done enough." For me, 1968 entailed a coming to consciousness more than a time of action.

I entered Rutgers College in the autumn 1967. Politically, I already leaned left. I had marched against conservative Republican Barry Goldwater with civil rights groups, but I was no radical. I imagined myself going on to law school and entering politics as a liberal Democrat. My grandparents and parents were social democrats who had instilled in me an instinctive hostility to racism and oppression. But I was no "red-diaper baby." Nor was I a cultural radical. I appreciated my parents and their generation. They had lived the Depression, fought the "good war," and done their best to make decent lives for us.

Having spent time in Ecuador as an exchange student and having seen the poverty and oppression, I sympathized with Latin American revolutionaries. But convinced that the Soviets were imperialists, I hesitated to oppose America's war in Vietnam. Nevertheless, by late summer 1967, even I had to admit that the United States was pursuing a neocolonial war and, thus, as soon as I arrived on campus I withdrew my name from the roster of the Reserve Officers Training Command.

At Rutgers, talk would inevitably turn to American history and foreign policy, the morality and constitutionality of America's involvement in Vietnam and how we might halt it or, at least, avoid serving in it. (Conservatives—many of whom successfully avoided the draft as well—try to portray my generation as a bunch of shirkers and subversives. But, besides trying to stay out of the army, we were also trying to resist imperialism, redeem an alternative vision of America, and cultivate an internationalism quite different from the corporate globalism that shapes our lives today.)

To be honest, whenever I think back to those days, I suffer feelings of ambivalence. I remember the aspirations and challenges, the urgency and excitement, *and* the fun, like the Country Joe & the Fish rock concert—"What Are We Fightin' For?"—organized by my social fraternity. I also well remember serving as associate editor of the Rutgers humor magazine, titled, in honor of the times, *The Lemming*—not to mention a few lemming-like romances. But memories of tragedy, loss, and defeat quickly overwhelm the nostalgia.

My recollection of American events repeatedly follows the same depressing trajectory. In my mind's eye, I see Lyndon Johnson on television announcing his withdrawal from the presidential campaign (March 31). I recall how, even as we celebrated our share in bringing an end to his administration, I felt strangely sorry for the man who had responded to the struggle for racial justice and equality and pushed through the Civil Rights and Voting Rights Acts.

I next remember the murder of Martin Luther King (April 4). I can still feel the sadness and anxiety of that night. It had to do not simply with the fear that the city's Black community would explode in rage (the dean's office advised us to stay on campus, preferably in our dorms), but, even more, with the fear that the nation's race relations would deteriorate still further. Then I recollect how, upon arriving at my parents' home after exams, I went to bed the night of the California primary election pleased that Bobby Kennedy had won (June 6), only to be awakened early next morning by my father with news of the assassination. In shock, I kept wondering "whither America?"

From there my thoughts rush ahead to the debacle of the Chicago Democratic Convention in August, and I hear again the news reports about violent confrontations between police and anti-war activists. Finally, I see myself back on campus, the morning after the November elections, standing in the shower, emotionally chilled, trying to fathom what had happened and to comprehend the words "President Nixon."

Recalling events elsewhere does not really help. Prague Spring greatly enthused and inspired me, but I cannot forget the Soviet tanks approaching over the horizon (August 20). I welcomed the apparent alliance of French students and workers, and lamented its absence in America. Like Johnson, Charles de Gaulle eventually retired, but all too many radical aspirations went unrealized. In Mexico, democratic forces gathered in favor of revitalizing the Mexican Revolution, but on the eve of the Olympiad the government suppressed a rally in the capital city's Plaza of the Three Cultures, and troops massacred almost 400 students and workers (October 2). In spite of talk of peace, Americans and Vietnamese continued to kill each other in the jungles of Southeast Asia.

I could close by reciting Dickens's opening lines to *A Tale of Two Cities*: "It was the best of times, it was the worst of times, it was the age of wisdom, it was the age of foolishness, it was the epoch of belief, it was the epoch of incredulity, it was the season of Light, it was the season of Darkness, it was the spring of hope, it was the winter of despair, we had everything before us, we had nothing before us, we were all going direct to Heaven, we were all going the other way."

But history did not stop. The struggles metamorphosed and, along with the continuing tragedies and ironies, change and even progress were achieved—inspired in part by the movements of 1968.

Chapter 11

1848 AND ALL THAT—
OR A VISION OF POETRY IN MOTION

In this sesquicentennial of *The Communist Manifesto*, I have a confession to make: I regularly try to disabuse myself of thinking like a Marxist, identifying with the labor movement, and believing in the promise of socialist democracy.

I continually force myself to confront the horrors of history, in particular those of the twentieth century, among them the nightmares of the now-collapsed Soviet regime. I do not fail to appreciate capitalism's productive wonders and consumer spectacles, and to cherish our liberal-democratic freedoms. Moreover, I immerse myself in the arguments of contemporary conservatives. I imagine what a pleasure it would be to accept the world as it is, to believe that the way things are is the way they ought to be—or, at least, to believe that they are the only way they can be. I even daydream about the commissions to be garnered if I disavowed the left.

Tragedy haunts the historical record; irony mocks humanity's best efforts. Capitalism affords tremendous powers and pleasures (for those who have the wherewithal); liberal democracy definitely is the finest form of political development (thus far). And conservatives not only write smartly, they also score good points (not to mention that I would welcome a greater public voice and bank account).

Nevertheless, however much I acknowledge these truths, I am unable to shed myself of Marxian thoughts, laborist commitments, and socialist hopes.

Some have argued that I suffer some intellectual malady: Perhaps nostalgia, a longing to recapture the past, a supposed time of confident socialist politics and laborist solidarities. Perhaps alienation, a desire to reorder society such that intellectuals not only study things but also rule

---

Originally appeared in *The Times Higher Education Supplement*, April 17, 1998.

them. Or maybe utopianism, a yearning to create a society of complete freedom, absolute equality, and total democracy. But they are wrong.

I do long for a more confident socialist politics and stronger solidarities among workers *and* among workers and intellectuals—but not simply for those of the past, marked in the former case by racial and gender hierarchies and in the latter by an acritical populism or more dangerous elitism. I do desire a reordering of society—but not to empower some refurbished ruling class. And I certainly do aspire to a freer, more equal and democratic future—though not to some unattainable or dangerous fantasy.

I readily admit to romanticism, radicalism, and optimism; but I don't think I suffer—at least not severely—from nostalgia, alienation, or utopianism. Overlooking pure stubbornness and/or stupidity, you might wonder: How can one continue to think like a Marxist, remain committed to working-class struggles, and still hold on to socialist visions?

In the light of history, and in the Talmudic fashion of my Jewish forebears, I reply: How can one *not* continue to ask Marxian questions? How can one *not* continue to side with labor? How can one *not* reaffirm socialist hopes and aspirations? Indeed, contrary to the respective philosophers of the end of history and *posthistoire*, has there been any time more in need and inviting of such questions, engagements, and visions?

Why ask Marxian questions? Political scientist Ellen Meiksins Wood contends: "For the first time, capitalism has become a truly universal system.... So Marx is more relevant than ever, because he, more effectively than any other human being then or now, devoted his life to explaining the systemic logic of capitalism."[1]

And, as she notes, in the *Manifesto* we find a most prophetic narrative of capitalist triumphalism: "The bourgeoisie has played a most revolutionary role in history.... The need of a constantly expanding market for its products chases the bourgeoisie over the whole surface of the globe. It must nestle everywhere, settle everywhere, establish connections everywhere.... In a word, it creates a world after its own image." Has there ever been an economist more prescient—or more poetic—than Marx?

Prescience and poetry aside, I think the continuing power of Marxian thought, with all its faults and neglects (of nationalism, race, and gender), lies in the political-economic *and* moral questions it poses. Where better to start an exploration of history than with the way in which people organize themselves to provide for their material and cultural needs and development? Specifically, where better to start than with a social order's relations of exploitation and oppression *and* the struggles engendered by them?

Of course, we need far more than Marx; but without Marxian questions how can we possibly make critical sense of history, no less the past quarter-century: Thatcherism and Reaganism, popular revolution in the Soviet world, corporate globalization, Asian economic crises and unrest . . . ?

Why support workers' struggles and the labor movement? Because, for a start, if we really do want to create freer, more equal and democratic societies, then we need to do so *democratically*. And history attests to working people's commitments and accomplishments.

Against the theses of Cold War social scientists and orthodox Marxists alike, recent generations of historians, working from the bottom up, have effectively demonstrated that the working class has been the class most devoted to democratic change and development.

Now, after 25 years of class war from above, fragmentation, and decomposition, the working classes are not simply more diverse, they are also recomposing themselves and reconstituting their social movements. In *Workers in a Lean World*, Kim Moody writes: "Like Mark Twain's proverbial death notice, the diagnosis [of labor's death] proved premature. By the mid-1990s the streets of continental Europe, Latin America, and parts of Asia were filled with hundreds of thousands of angry working people."[2]

And, once again, their campaigns are reinvigorating democratic politics as intellectuals realign themselves with reinvigorating labor movements. The struggle to extend and enrich democracy continues—globalization has merely raised the stakes.

Why cultivate socialist aspirations? Because, for all its corruptions and perversions, socialism represents the modern articulation of humanity's ancient dream of abolishing exploitation and oppression and creating social orders without overlords. Emerging in the wake of the Enlightenment, taking shape in the course of the Age of Revolution, and developing in relation to the making of labor movements, socialism—at its best—has served as the "prophetic memory" of working people's aspirations to freedom, equality, and democracy.

And just consider: Though democratic life remains constrained and tested, who does not publicly revere democracy, or at least defer to it as an ideal? Though inequalities persist and grow, who publicly recites the classical conservative defenses of inequality? Though capital and the market prevail, who actually trusts corporate power, global or otherwise?

Whatever the politics of the likes of Britain's "New Labour" and the Third Way, we should not fail to comprehend what recent left political victories mean. Against all the best efforts to convince them otherwise, working people and the middle classes refuse to abandon the hope that societies of greater freedom, equality, and democracy might yet be made. History is not over.

Conservatives are not oblivious. In the wake of their recent electoral defeats in Western Europe and the United States, New Rightists convened an International Conservative Convention, co-hosted by Margaret Thatcher and William F. Buckley, to consider what the neoconservative *Weekly Standard* called the "Worldwide Conservative Crack-Up."[3]

We should be so lucky. Still, I can't help thinking they, too, have read their Marx.

Chapter 12

THE THIRD WAY IS THE WRONG WAY

After 20 years of New Right ascendance, Western European voters have returned the parties of the left—such as Labour in Britain, the Socialists in France, and the Social Democrats, in coalition with the Greens, in Germany—to political power.

Do these leftist victories represent the reemergence of "class politics" in Europe? Will these new governments attempt to subordinate the market and capital to the public good and the needs of working people?

The left's electoral victories clearly reflect a growing popular rejection of policies favoring corporate priorities and the hegemony of the market. Nevertheless, we should not soon expect to hear calls for "power to the people" or to "keep the red flag flying," at least not from today's Euro-left leaders. As the corporate media fondly reassure us: Whatever their supporters might desire, the "*center*-left" likes of Britain's Tony Blair, France's Lionel Jospin, and Germany's Gerhard Schroder represent a dramatic *break* from the past and the advent of a new "Third Way" politics.

Rarely used with any precision, Third Way basically refers to a politics and governing vision (supposedly) alternative both to the market fundamentalism of the right *and* to the statism of the socialist tradition. Curiously, the term seems to have originated on this side of the Atlantic. Campaign consultant Dick Morris recounts how, in the wake of the Republican triumphs in the 1994 congressional elections, he advised President Clinton to "triangulate, create a third position, not just in between the old positions of the two parties, but above them as well." Morris claims he suggested "triangulation as a way to change, not abandon, the Democratic party." Soon after, Clinton began to speak of having discovered a "third way" for government, beyond Reagan Republicanism and New Deal/Great Society liberalism.

Of course, Clinton didn't have to go very far to distance himself from liberalism; but, given his signing of the so-called Welfare Reform Act, it's

---

Originally appeared in a somewhat shorter version in *The Progressive*, August 1999.

hard to tell how his Third Way fundamentally differs from the Republican way. Meanwhile, his supporters in the Democratic Leadership Council (DLC), the business-oriented right wing of the party, have taken to touting the Third Way as a "progressive global political movement" attuned to the "new challenges of the Information Age."

Tony Blair, the Third Way's foremost European champion, appropriated and inflated such rhetoric for his "New Labour" campaign (shades of Clinton's "New Democrats") and succeeded in keeping it aloft long enough to soundly defeat the Tories at the May 1997 elections. Though Blair never spelled out exactly what the Third Way entails, he cleverly promoted it by recruiting to his campaign not only some very sharp public relations folk but also some very impressive intellectuals, the most prominent among them being Anthony Giddens, then professor of sociology at Cambridge University.

Giddens has established himself as one of the world's leading social theorists. His first major work, *Capitalism and Modern Social Theory*, firmly secured Karl Marx, Max Weber, and Emile Durkheim as the founding trinity of modern sociology.[1] Thereafter, in a string of books, he developed "structuration theory" as an alternative to the sterile theoretical debates between sociologists who emphasized "structural determinations" and those who emphasized "social action." And, in the 1990s, he took to the pages of the political weeklies to write about issues like inequality, the family, and the welfare state.

In 1994 Giddens published *Beyond Left and Right: The Future of Radical Politics*,[2] which made him appear a natural candidate to help a young, rising left politician develop a fresh political vision. Further adding to his public stature, in 1996 Giddens was elected director of the prestigious London School of Economics, to which he quickly recruited a host of new academic celebrities eager to advise a new "New Labour" government. Prolific, and seemingly indefatigable, Giddens has had the responsibility of trying to inject some intellectual substance into Blair's rhetoric.

When I first heard that Giddens had written *The Third Way: The Renewal of Social Democracy*,[3] I hoped he had injected some radical-democratic character into Third Way thinking. Since in his previous writings he regularly referred to the work of the late British sociologist T. H. Marshall—especially Marshall's classic work, *Citizenship and Social Class* (first presented as lectures in 1947)[4]—I began to imagine that Giddens might have drawn critically on Marshall's historical perspective and ideas.

Marshall offered a grand narrative of the development of rights and equality. Debate continues over whether he had in mind an evolutionary or struggle-based process. Nevertheless, Marshall suggested we comprehend the making of modern democratic history in terms of three waves or advances in the securing of the rights of citizenship. The first entails the establishment of civil rights, most significantly freedom of speech and religion, the right to own property, and equality before the law. The second involves political rights, specifically the right to vote and engage in political affairs. And the third comprises social rights, such as rights to education, healthcare, and welfare.

Social rights are far from secure, especially after 20 years of New Right rule, and, in any case, they remain relatively underdeveloped here in the United States compared to Western Europe, most notably so in comparison to the Scandinavian countries. I figured Giddens had realized the time had come to call for a fresh advance, the development of a struggle for economic rights, that is, democratic control of the corporate economy (in which case he might have titled his book "The Fourth Wave").

The groundwork for a democratic economy already exists in various European countries where workers' representatives sit on corporate boards and, in yet another fashion, here in the United States, where we established the Occupational Safety and Health Administration (OSHA) and Environmental Protection Agency (EPA) to challenge, delimit, and control corporate power and authority. I hoped that Giddens, if not as a socialist, then in the spirit of the sixties, had renewed the call for democratic participation and/or workers' control. Unfortunately, I was wrong.

Reading Giddens's *The Third Way*, I found myself recalling radical sociologist C. Wright Mills on intellectuals and politics. Mills insisted that those of us committed to democracy should aspire neither to the role of philosopher-king nor to that of adviser to the king—for democratic development requires *democratic* development. Rather, a democratic intellectual should always seek to challenge the powerful and cultivate democratic publics.

Sadly, Giddens has aligned himself with the politically powerful and written a book that defers to the ideological claims of the right and the political economy of global capital. More than once, he resorts to what *Nation* writer Daniel Singer calls TINA—Margaret "Iron Lady" Thatcher's assertion that "there is no alternative" to capitalism.[5]

At the same time, Giddens reduces the politics and aspirations of the left to "helping citizens pilot their way through the major revolutions of our time: *globalization*, *transformations in personal life*, and our *relationship to nature*."

Admittedly, he acknowledges that the pursuit of equality, social justice, and an "emancipatory politics" must remain at the heart of social-democratic politics; but he reconstrues equality to mean merely "inclusion" in the social mainstream and "emancipation" to mean simply having the wherewithal to participate in it (such as healthcare and lifelong learning opportunities). For too many folk, such things would represent dramatic improvements, but they hardly represent an inspired politics of radical change. Still, Giddens must fear it all sounds too demanding for our economic elites, for he makes sure to advance a new motto for the new politics: "No rights without responsibilities." In the end, I find it hard to distinguish such thinking from the "welfare-to-work" politics of Wisconsin's Republican Governor, Tommy Thompson.

Giddens judiciously sprinkles his text with references to democracy. His most radical statement in this respect is "no authority without democracy." However, Giddens uncharacteristically forgets history. Democracy does not just happen. To secure, preserve, and enhance it requires popular struggle, organization, and diligence. But, aside from a few words about "citizen initiative groups," Giddens makes no reference to real social struggles. And he is platitudinously vague as to what Third Way democracy would look and feel like.

In the face of concentrating corporate power, Giddens completely ignores the question of the power and authority of capital and how it threatens democratic life. And he essentially dismisses the possibility of renewing working-class organization. Presumably, Third Way democracy will involve active but limited government by morally well-intentioned politicians, pursuing policies fabricated by elite academic intellectuals, in favor of empowering highly individualized citizens to be all that each one of them can be.

Giddens avers that while global free trade and finance cannot be controlled, they must at least be regulated (he has held lengthy conversations with international financier George Soros). But Giddens's references to possible multinational regulating agencies never really get at matters of power and inequality. Though my own sympathies lie with "workers of the world unite," in view of such global elitism I can readily understand why Pat Buchanan's neo-isolationism seems appealing to many of my fellow Americans.

Arguably, Tony Blair's media-bloated campaigns and Tony Giddens's narrow, deferential vision for social democracy represent not simply the acceptance of the triumph of capital but also the Americanization of European politics and ideas. Thus, it greatly behooves the American left, in particular, to articulate a truly progressive alternative vision and politics, grounded in the better part of our history, the radical-democratic tradition of "We, the People."

Chapter 13

SIGNS OF LIFE: AMERICAN HISTORY, MEMORY, AND DEMOCRACY

In October 1999, on the eve of the new century, we lost another link to the Revolution of 1776 when work crews on the St. John's College campus in Annapolis, Maryland, brought down the last of the original Liberty Trees. Beneath those trees, Americans fashioned a liberation movement against British rule and turned themselves into citizens. The trees became historic symbols of our nation's struggle for independence. Unfortunately, having already endured terrible decay, the remaining specimen suffered fatal damage in Hurricane Floyd. Specialists could not save it.

The Liberty Tree's removal saddened me, but my sadness had to do with more than the demise of a great tree. The tree's final destruction seemed a warning about the condition of American public life and the prospects for radical-democratic politics. The words of one arborist sounded like a metaphor for the state of American democracy: "The entire tree now consists of a hollow shell of wood."[1]

We have witnessed conservative political ascendance, expanding corporate hegemony, and the subjection of public goods to market priorities. The rich have grown grossly richer and working people and the poor poorer. And we of the democratic left find ourselves relegated to the margins of public debate. Even the most foolish of optimists could not fail to appreciate the daunting character of the challenges we face.

Yet we should not allow our perennial pessimism of the intellect to obscure critical signs of democratic life. If we look closely, we will find significant grounds for hope and action. I leave it to my activist comrades to survey our social movements and render prognoses for their reinvigoration. I write as a historian, one who studies and obsesses about American historical memory, consciousness, and imagination, and about the grand narrative by which we understand and speak of ourselves as a people.

Originally appeared in *Democratic Left*, vol. 29, no. 1, 2000. Reprinted by permission of Democratic Socialists of America.

I obsess with good cause, for, as Benjamin Barber observes in *An Aristocracy of Everyone*, "the story we tell about ourselves defines not just us but our possibilities." Forget the postmodernists' hostilities toward grand narrative. As Joyce Appleby, Lynn Hunt, and Margaret Jacob point out in *Telling the Truth About History*: "Narratives and meta-narratives are the kinds of stories that make action in the world possible. They make action possible because they make it meaningful."[2]

For the past 30 years radical historians have engaged in a struggle to shape—better, *re*shape—America's historical understandings. Inspired by the movements of the day, many of us entered the historical profession intent upon recovering the lives and struggles that our predecessors had ignored *and* refashioning the prevailing grand narrative in light of those recoveries. We hoped to contribute to the reformation of public thinking, deliberation, and agency—and, thereby, to the very making of history. We accomplished volumes, and our labors did not go unappreciated, most notably by the right.

The very formation and rise of the New Right entailed the aggressive use and abuse of history. Eager to both combat our work and promote a new conservative understanding of past, present, and possible futures, the Reagan Republicans, in their pursuit of the culture wars, regularly targeted for attack our teaching and research. The climax of their campaigns came in the battles over the National Standards for History. Commissioned by the Bush administration, but published during the Clinton presidency, the standards did not fulfill conservative ambitions. In fact, they tendered a far more critical and promising set of ideas than the right could stomach, and conservatives quickly sought to drown them in a flood of hostile rhetoric. The ensuing conflict, from the AM radio airwaves to the floor of Congress, clearly demonstrated the right's public power and influence, but also the left's strength in academe.[3]

However climactic the standards conflict, the issue of the grand narrative persists. Indeed, it reverberates throughout American public *and* private life. Historians naturally concern themselves with the question. In 1981 Herbert Gutman challenged us to remember our original aspirations and take the lead in refashioning America's narrative, to more effectively connect with our fellow citizens. In the 20 years since, many other, diverse historians have repeated Gutman's call (myself included). African American scholar Nathan Huggins insists in *Revelations: American History, American Myths* that "we should not forget that the end of our study of history is no less than the reconstruction of American history. . . . We all need to be calling for a new narrative. . . . It is especially important for Afro-American historians." Introducing *Born for Liberty: A History of Women in America*, Sara Evans writes: "Now we have many histories, and the historian's task is to integrate these experiences into the dominant narrative of the American past, the main story we tell ourselves about who we have been as a nation." And Appleby, Hunt, and Jacob reaffirm that we "now confront the task of creating a new narrative framework."[4]

Not just historians agonize. In *The One and the Many*, professor of religious studies Martin E. Marty addresses the problem of "our common story." Poet laureate Robert Pinsky commences "Poetry and American Memory" by stating that "though the United States is assuredly a great nation, the question remains open whether we are a great people or are still engaged in the undertaking of becoming a great people. A people is defined and unified not by blood but by shared memory," and he goes on to "seek a vision of our future in the poetry of our past." And in *The Real American Dream*, literary scholar Andrew Delbanco starts, as well, by asserting the necessity of a narrative and then advances one focusing on Americans' changing beliefs about hope and transcendence.[5]

Nor does the matter agitate merely academics. In *The Party's Not Over Yet*, public policy analyst Jeff Faux decries that we have become trapped in a conservative public discourse, and he urges liberals and leftists to develop a new narrative to escape the right's hold. Former conservative Michael Lind ponders "The Liberal Search for a Usable Past" and makes a major effort to outline a new grand narrative in *The Next American Nation*. More entertaining, but no less serious, Steve Darnall and Alex Ross have authored and illustrated *U.S.*, a two-volume comic book in which a confused Uncle Sam seeks to "remember his true identity" while memories and voices propel him on a time-travel journey through America's past. Hell, even the conservative faithful feel apprehensive. One vocal participant at a January 1999 Republican gathering called "The Weekend" implored the party's leadership to "tell a better story . . . the story of what America is supposed to be, the story of what America is going to be."[6]

Anxiety about America's grand narrative seems universal. Reacting to claims that Americans have no interest in the past, historians Roy Rosenzweig and David Thelen surveyed and interviewed 1500 people about their "connection to the past and its continuing influence on their present lives and hopes." As Rosenzweig and Thelen report in *The Presence of the Past*, they discovered that while Americans take their relationship to the past quite seriously and, in their respective ways, actively seek to engage history, most do not readily connect their own intimate pasts with any overarching collective or national story. Americans do, however, recognize and affirm the value and import of just such a narrative.[7]

We definitely should not fail to attend to and appreciate our conservative compatriots' continuing anxieties and fears regarding the grand narrative. Their writings may tell us things we have forgotten or not even realized—at the least, they should serve to remind us that the struggle continues.

In "American Epic: Then and Now," neoconservative Nathan Glazer defines an epic as "a story recounting great deeds." Observing how "epic . . . comes up everywhere when one thinks about America," he rightly connects "America as epic" to the idea of "American exceptionalism." He notes that the epic which long dominated American consciousness spoke of "the American idea . . . the American creed . . . the American dream . . . Manifest Destiny." It emphasized "the newness, the vastness, the openness of America—the freedom thereby granted Americans." Moreover, it told a story of "Americanization"—of later immigrant generations pursuing the dream and, in the process, transforming themselves into Americans.

Yet, Glazer explains, in recent decades a more problematic narrative has superseded the original: "The one grand epic has been succeeded by many fragmentary little epics. . . . The new fragments create epics that celebrate the destruction of a domineering and false oneness by a manyness; and we wonder whether that means also the fragmenting of a nation." Glazer does not discount how the narrative suppressed or marginalized experiences, nor does he yearn for restoration of the older epic. Nonetheless, his words express loss and lamentation. He relates a tale of declension. He mourns the fragmentation of a grand unifying epic and distresses over what it might portend: "Of course, we can live without an American epic. But that does diminish us, and it is easy to understand why some of our poets, artists, writers, and historians keep on trying."[8]

One does not have to subscribe to Glazer's politics to sympathize with his general argument. However, his apparently reasonable sentiments deceive. While sideswiping the academic left for promoting race, ethnic, and women studies, he refuses to acknowledge the work of a generation of historians who have directed their efforts at transforming, not destroying, America's grand narrative. By way of omission, Glazer essentially repeats Arthur Schlesinger, Jr.'s accusations in *The Disuniting of America* that the left advocates fragmentation, a claim that necessarily involved conflating the work of Afro-centrists and other particularists with that of the academic left as a whole.[9]

Fragmentation probably *does* disturb Glazer and his ilk, but it disturbs many of us, too. Perhaps conservatives worry as they do because radical-democratic historians not only have aspired to refashion the American epic but have also started doing so. And as much as we recognize the tragic and ironic character of the making of America and the diverse experiences involved in it, our works articulate a grand narrative of struggle, progress, and promise. Consider, as examples, the American Social History Project's

Who Built America?, Ronald Takaki's *A Different Mirror*, and Eric Foner's *The Story of American Freedom*. Concluding his book, Takaki writes: "As Americans, we originally came from many different shores, and our diversity has been at the center of the making of modern America. While our stories contain the memories of different communities, together they inscribe a larger narrative."[10]

If our efforts perturb them so, conservatives must get all the more distressed to learn that our work actually seems to have had an influence. We have far from triumphed, but—contrary to what we ourselves have usually assumed—it appears we have had some impact on recent generations' historical memory, consciousness, and imagination. The 1996 Survey of American Political Culture shows that the overwhelming majority of our fellow citizens recognize that the nation "expanded at the cost of much suffering," "betrayed its principles by the cruel mistreatment of Blacks and American Indians," and "subjected women to a male-dominated culture." At the same time, Americans continue to subscribe to the "American creed" —understood as a "commitment to liberty, equality, democracy, and the 'melting pot' theory of national identity"—*and* they continue to understand the nation's history as entailing the "expansion of freedom." Furthermore, they want that grand narrative and those critical understandings taught to their children.[11] Note the success of Joy Hakim's *A History of US*, a 10-volume study of American history for children and young people. Its truly extraordinary sales history clearly indicates the popular demand for a well-written critical interpretation of American experience. Parents want their children to learn America's exceptional story.[12]

Like our fellow citizens, we must avoid one-dimensional thinking. Inspired by the revolutionary promise of the Founders, the American radical tradition has imbued American life with experiences, images, and figures that resonate across historical generations. Don't accuse me of praising the corporately owned media, but I cannot resist recounting my surprise and delight in coming across a recent *Life Magazine* "collector's edition." The editors had dedicated the issue to "Celebrating Our Heroes." *And* their 25-member "Hall of Heroes" included 16 progressives and radicals: Abraham Lincoln, Franklin Roosevelt, Eleanor Roosevelt, Martin Luther King, Jr., Tecumseh, Thomas Jefferson, Margaret Sanger, Harriet Tubman, Frederick Douglass, Susan B. Anthony, Jane Addams, Cesar Chavez, Helen Keller, Rachel Carson, Jacob Riis, and Mother Jones.[13]

We need to take seriously this complex of anxious yearnings and democratic memories. They represent critical possibilities *and* resources. If we don't engage them, others will. In addition to revealing that Americans endorse a progressive view of American history, the Survey of American

Political Culture registered pervasive uneasiness and concern about America's institutions and the future: "Hardly anyone, it seems, is chanting a slogan of 'progress' anymore."[14]

Unfortunately, while historians can write epic works, they cannot alone craft grand narratives. The democratic left needs not only to write good history but also to make it. I just hope that, along with the obstacles, we appreciate the possibilities.

I opened with the death of the last Liberty Tree. I close on a couple of more promising notes. In the course of the same year, the federal government announced that as a consequence of the banning of DDT and the passage of the Endangered Species Act back in the early 1970s, the American bald eagle no longer stands on the brink of extinction. And the Smithsonian Institution initiated a major restoration project of the flag that flew over Fort McHenry in Baltimore in 1814 and inspired Francis Scott Key to compose *The Star Spangled Banner*. These attest that in some instances, at least, collective public effort can reverse the seemingly inevitable.[15]

*Affairs
Literary*

Chapter 14

IN BOOKSTORES, BIGGER CAN BE BETTER

I respond to a bookstore like a gambler to a casino. And for many years my Las Vegas was London. Indeed, ever since my days as a postgraduate student in London, I could never sleep on the overnight flights back to Britain. I'd stay awake, anxiously planning where to initiate the day's action: Dillons, Colletts, Foyles, The Economist, Compendium, *or* Central Books for a look at the secondhand collection? Ah, the good old days . . . My wife's college friend and former flatmate would pick up Lorna and the girls at Heathrow, and I would immediately head by train for the first bookshop on my list. Between trips, I would dream about those rooms of books.

Much has changed. Admittedly, London now has Waterstone's. But, sadly, Colletts and Central have closed up shop, The Economist has become a shadow of its former self, Dillons has had serious troubles, and Foyles seems even nastier than ever. Honestly, while I still look forward eagerly to visiting London—and still spend too much time in the bookshops—it just isn't the same.

Yet, before you think me merely nostalgic and ready to take off in a tirade against the corporate takeover of bookselling and everything else, let me say that while the London scene ain't what it used to be, neither— thank goodness!—is the American.

As those of you Britons who have visited the States know, what we Americans have been willing to call bookstores weren't really *book*stores at all. Sure, a city like New York seems always to have had Barnes & Noble for new and publishers' cleared titles and The Strand for used books; and the San Francisco Bay Area has had Cody's and Moe's. And, yes, every bigtime university town (which Green Bay is not) has had a campus co-op stocked with workbooks, textbooks, and a selection of real books, plus an assortment of eccentric new and secondhand booksellers.

Nevertheless, you'd have had a really hard time finding a good bookstore when the skyscrapers or ivory towers no longer stood on the hori-

---

Originally appeared in *The Times Higher Education Supplement*, February 23, 1996.

zon. Of course there were exceptions, but the independently owned, main-street shops of small-town America were mostly purveyors of greeting cards, magazines, calendars, bestsellers, and how-to books. Perhaps they were welcoming places, but I feel confident in saying that those portrayed in Hollywood films were always more interesting, cavernous, and well stocked than the real ones.

The suburban scene presented an equally bleak picture. Recognizing the commercial possibilities, in the 1960s and 1970s "chain" bookstores spread and installed themselves in the new shopping malls. Offering the literary counterparts to the jeans, cassettes, and cosmetics on sale elsewhere in those sparkling but culturally antiseptic environments, they provided merchandise that was just as bland and packaged. Given the apparently far greater space, they were able to entice customers away from downtown with the newest picture books, the latest biographies and pathographies, and the slickest self-help volumes on "relationships" and New Age business and religion.

Desperately, one would search the shelves, hoping to find something of value. There were now more and bigger stores, but things had hardly improved. Actually, they had gotten worse, for at least the downtown bookseller had had a sincere interest in books. The staff in the mall knew less and didn't seem at all ashamed by their ignorance. All decisions were made at corporate headquarters.

As evil as corporate capitalism can be, sometimes it surprises. Recently—via the competitive enterprise of two companies, Borders and Barnes & Noble—it has seen fit to create a new kind of American bookshop, the "superstore." A truly marvelous development on the otherwise depressing corporate-cultural landscape of '90s America, superstores are popping up in city centers and suburbia alike. They are most remarkable places. From a distance they would seem to be simply bigger versions of the mall stores but, trust me, they are not. Arguably, they are more like the bookstores of our nostalgic past, but on a giant scale.

For a start, they regularly stock a whopping 100,000 titles, including books in every possible subject from astronomy to zoology, classics to cultural studies. The history and social science sections alone contain more volumes than an entire chain-store outlet. Additionally, the superstore's newspaper and magazine racks appeal to every taste imaginable and, amazingly, they usually include several dedicated specifically to political and literary journals traditionally associated with the likes of "intellectuals" (such as the *New York Review of Books*, *London Review of Books*, and *Times Literary Supplement*). Plus the underpaid but interested, college-educated staff usually know about the titles sitting in their respective sections and, in any case, computers can quickly tell them what they need to know.

Moreover, while you can enjoy these emporia on your own *and* for many hours (for they stay open very late and have "comfy chairs" and couches to settle in for proper browsing), they also welcome families and social outings. A few times each week, such stores host promotional events like talks, readings, and even small concerts, and I have visited several places where book groups have formed and hold weekly discussions, occasionally with a visiting author. Moreover, every store has a children's section with its own scaled-down furniture and storytelling corner where on weekends you'll find a staff member or guest storyteller performing. Presumably in an effort to appeal to somewhat older kids, I have even read of singles' gatherings at superstores.

There is more. Superstores often have a music floor where you not only can browse but also, as in the stores of old, pick up headphones to hear the latest recordings before you buy (something I hadn't seen since my first visit to Edinburgh, Scotland, almost 20 years ago). To top it all off, superstores have built-in coffee bars where you can get a bite to eat with your favorite flavor of coffee, juice, or soda (the yuppie version of the teashop that used to be situated alongside every good English bookshop).

I have not gone soft on corporate capitalism. I know the criticisms of the superstores but, in contrast to most other commercial developments, I love this one. I have read reports that they are driving the remaining independent shops out of business. Yet such reports usually refer to urban areas where a surfeit of good bookstores prevail; not to mention that certain independent shops have successfully confronted the invasion of superstores by transforming themselves into the same kind of grand-scale literary venue. At the same time (and I say it with a smile), I know that mall stores, too, are going under because they can't compete with nearby superstores. Also, I should note that superstores pay their staff no worse than the independents and are probably more likely to provide employee benefits like health insurance (a crucial thing in this country).

Neither am I naive. I know that many of the shoppers entering superstores merely do so in search of the same pop reading they'd have looked for in the mall stores. Still, in the superstores they might pick up something original (besides a date), or they might stop in on an evening when a good writer is speaking.

I continue to dream of London. But I have begun to fantasize about possibilities closer to home. By way of the local Oneida and Menominee Indian tribes, we now have gaming casinos and slot machines in northeast Wisconsin. Why not, I figure, a really *super* bookstore?

Chapter 15

READING THE RIGHT—
OR IT'S A DIRTY JOB, BUT . . .

My university colleagues often ask me how I can bear to read conservative writings as much as I do—and, when they do, it's often followed by someone joking about my having "gone over to the other side." I used to just laugh and reply that "it's a dirty job, but somebody has to do it." However, I now recognize there's more to it than that.

Don't get the wrong idea. Don't even begin to imagine that I have donned new colors and switched from red to white. No, my left-wing politics haven't changed. But, in addition to believing that someone has to keep an eye on the right, I now also realize the value of reading conservatives. Indeed, I actually have come to enjoy doing so.

I first started looking seriously into conservative speechifying and writing in the early 1980s, in the wake of the electoral triumphs of Ronald Reagan (1980) and Margaret Thatcher (1979). As a historian and sociologist, it fascinated me how those two and their political comrades effectively used *and* abused their respective national pasts. At the very outset, they used the "past" to harness and align their diverse constituencies—ranging, in the U.S. case, from corporate free-marketeers to Christian fundamentalists. Beyond that, they did so to mobilize popular support and build a conservative consensus or, more critically stated, conservative hegemony.

My own generation had taken up scholarly labors to redeem popular struggles past and present "from the bottom up" and to revise the prevailing governing narratives of history in the light of those recoveries. We aspired to develop critical historical memory, consciousness, and imagination amongst our fellow citizens. In that fashion, we hoped to contribute to the extension and deepening of liberty, equality, and democracy. And

---

These reflections relate, in particular, to my writing of the column "It's a Dirty Job, But . . . : A Quarterly Look at Conservative Periodicals and Pundits" for *Democratic Left*, the magazine of Democratic Socialists of America, during 1997.

we accomplished volumes. Yet, for all our work, we apparently have yet to have the kind of persuasive impact that Reagan and Thatcher had with their nostalgic renditions of America's and Britain's pasts [or have we?— see Chapter 13].

Most of my own work in the 1980s treated the British Marxist historical tradition,[1] and my family and I regularly made trips to Britain both for research purposes and to visit my wife's family. Traveling back and forth across the Atlantic, one could not help but notice the similarities between Reaganism and Thatcherism, including the emphases placed on matters "historical" by their respective Republican and Tory proponents. Increasingly, I turned my scholarly attentions to the right, convinced that my colleagues and I were failing to appreciate the New Right's ideas, ambitions, *and* appeal to our fellow citizens. Given the conservatives' political ascendance and hegemonic ambitions, I felt we needed to learn as much as we could about them.

In the 1980s, I began to prepare a book on the crisis of history and the American and British New Rights' uses and abuses of the past.[2] I hung a photo on the wall above my desk of Reagan and Thatcher strolling together happily in the White House Rose Garden. Seeing their smiling faces, while knowing the devastation and hardship their policies had wrought, infuriated me and inspired me to write. I read their speeches, and I admired their skills and audacity.

Furthermore, then and since I have made it a point of keeping up with the American conservative punditocracy.[3] I have endured the television talk shows its cadres dominate and subjected myself to the numerous well-funded, extra-academic periodicals for which they write. I have surveyed William F. Buckley's *National Review*, the flagship conservative weekly. I have despised and relished *American Spectator* for its *National Enquirer*–like exposés (and in the Age of Clinton it has never lacked for dirt). And I have perused the newer and newsier, Rupert Murdoch–sponsored, William Kristol–edited, "inside-the-beltway magazine" *Weekly Standard*.

I have studied the many symposia—like "The Future of Conservatism" and "Is Affirmative Action on the Way Out? Should It Be?"—organized by *Commentary*, the foremost of the neoconservative monthlies (edited for many years by the writer, Norman Podhoretz). I have followed the public affairs discussions in *American Enterprise*, the magazine of the Fortune 500–endowed American Enterprise Institute, and *Policy Review*, the Heritage Foundation's journal of ideas. And I have scrutinized many an essay in *Public Interest*, the premier neoconservative social science journal (edited by Irving Kristol and Nathan Glazer), and *National Interest*, the foremost neoconservative international affairs journal (which in 1989 published Francis Fukuyama's "The End of History?").

Also, I have regularly checked the contents of *First Things*, a "religion and public affairs" magazine, *New Criterion*, a cultural and arts monthly, and the originally radical but now conservative *Partisan Review* for critical essays on higher education and the scholarship of the academic left. Hell, I even keep an eye on *Chronicles*, the paleo-conservative monthly published by the Rockford Institute, which postures as populist but smells of traditional elitism and worse.

It frustrated me that so many of my colleagues and comrades on the left had avoided taking the right's ideas and thinking seriously, even after years of New Right governance and political dominance. If nothing else, I have found the right's words angering *and* invigorating of critical thought and action.

Nevertheless, reading the right has done more than incite me. It has educated me. For a start, conservative public intellectuals write in an understandable and accessible prose. Even wordsmiths like William F. Buckley, Jr., seem to know how not to alienate their readers. Too many of my colleagues on the left have taken to writing in ways that I am not sure they themselves understand. Political defeats, academic retreats, and postmodern fetes seem to have dulled too many of our best minds and pens.

Writing clearly, American conservatives have appealed to Americans' shared values and positioned themselves as their champions (even as they manipulate and pervert them). They have spoken the language of both liberty and freedom, and family and security (even as their policies undermine all of them). They have offered hope and promise (even as they advantage the most privileged and punish the weakest). Of course, the New Right coalition has remained contradictory and fragile. And those very contradictions have helped to limit the right's appeal. How could they ever truly reconcile market values and family values? Fortunately, Americans are not stupid. They are not eager to hand everything over to the dictates of the market or the Christian Coalition (at least, not so far).

Reading the right, I have become all the more aware of the persistent divisions among conservatives, neoconservatives, paleo-conservatives, and the religious right. I have learned about their tensions and antagonisms (which are sharp and occasionally have engendered serious ideological conflict, as happened, for example, when the editors of *First Things* ran a symposium that essentially challenged the legitimacy of the United States government).[4] Doing so has given me some satisfaction, as well as a bit of hope that the right might actually self-destruct.

I also have learned what has made conservatives nervous, not only nervous about each other but also, surprisingly, nervous about the remnants of the left. Conservatives know well of America's radical-democratic impulse and of Americans' commitment not only to liberty but also to justice, equality, and democracy. They know that Americans have accommodated themselves to the conservative consensus, not truly endorsed it. Thus, conservatives have remained ever sensitive to and vigilant about developments on the left and to what they might portend, most notably, of late, the renewal of the labor movement and the electoral victories of European social-democratic parties. Ironically, perhaps, reading the right has often served to reassure me that the left survives and might yet again make progressive history.[5]

I naturally welcomed philosopher Ronald Aronson's proposal to Democratic Socialists of America (DSA) to establish the Center for Democratic Values. Aronson has contended, as I have, that the left continually has failed to face up to the ideas of the right. So, in 1996, he proposed that we pursue a project dedicated not only to studying developments on the right but also to directly engaging conservatives in public argument. With DSA's support, Aronson recruited a number of us to serve as an advisory board and set about organizing a major event to inaugurate the Center.

We held our first conference—"Arguing with the Right"—in November 1997 in Columbus, Ohio. The highlight of the meeting—taped and later broadcast nationally on C-SPAN—was a debate between left and right. Socialist-feminist writer Barbara Ehrenreich and Harvard African American studies scholar Cornel West represented the left (not liberalism, but the radical-democratic left) and Stuart Butler of the Heritage Foundation and David Frum, a rising star among neoconservative columnists, represented the right. The event proved a major success and smaller events ensued; but, unfortunately, a lack of financial resources has limited the Center's ability to make the most of its successes. Still, it represents a model for future efforts.

I confess to liking some of the arguments I have encountered in the pages of the conservative press. For example, though a number of his references aggravated me, I applauded *Weekly Standard* senior editor David Brooks when he chastised his fellow conservatives for failing to develop a new vision of American greatness and a grand civic project to embody it.[6] At the same time, I wondered and worried what my colleagues and I on the left would have to offer. (In another vein, even if I did not support impeaching Bill Clinton, and even if my political criticisms were contrary to those rendered by the folks on the right, I could not help but get a kick out of the conservatives' diatribes against him and his administration.)

In fact—dare I admit it?—I have even made a couple of friends among the neoconservative columnists. Conversations have been insightful, challenging, and—I feel almost guilty saying it—fun. To hold my ground, I have had to sharpen my thinking in the course of our exchanges. Occasionally, we have even joked about converting each other to the other's politics (a most improbable possibility, though I sense they're weakening).

If the American left intends to challenge the order and consensus of the day, we will need to know what we're up against and what's on the minds of our antagonists. They command public debate—we do not. Without deferring, or following their every example, we surely have lots to learn from the conservatives—about them, about America, and about ourselves.

Chapter 16

WRITING FOR KIDS—
OR IN PRAISE OF JUVENILE EFFORTS

The Christmas and Chanukah holiday season seems a most appropriate time to highlight the American academy's latest literary movement. Apparently, more and more professors are giving up their traditional snobbishness toward things "childish" and taking up commissions to author books for kids and "young adults" (12–18 year olds).

When I accepted an invitation from Oxford University Press (OUP) to write a young people's biography of the late-eighteenth-century revolutionary Thomas Paine, I naively and immodestly had envisioned myself an intellectual rebel or pioneer. However, when I later asked my editor Nancy Toff, director of children's publishing at OUP here in the United States, which other university folk she had recruited to write histories, she happily replied with a long and impressive list of scholars and subjects.

As series editors, she had lined up the likes of Jon Butler and Harry Stout of Yale for Religion in American Life, Robin Kelley of New York University and Earl Lewis of Michigan for African American History, and Nancy Cott of Yale for American Women's History. And her stable of writers included Stephen Stein of Indiana on *Alternative American Religions*, Albert Raboteau of Princeton on *African American Religion*, Allan Winkler of Miami on *The Cold War*, Marilyn Young of New York University on *The Vietnam War*, Roger Daniels of Cincinnati on *American Immigration*, John Demos of Yale on *Native American Women*, and Elaine Tyler May of Minnesota on *American Women, 1940–1961*. I may not have been the rebel I had believed myself to be; but, whatever I was, I was in good company.

As we know, university faculty have long subscribed to a rather narrow concept of academic publishing. Only recently have professors eagerly sought to reach extra-academic audiences. Presumably, tenure and promotion will forever hang on refereed-journal articles and university press

---

Originally appeared in *The Times Higher Education Supplement*, January 1, 1999.

monographs. Nevertheless, something is clearly happening when, all of a sudden, leading scholars aspire to write not just for their peers and students but also for precollege adolescents. My own enlistment as a children's author was pure serendipity. But perhaps my reasons for signing on were not so unusual.

I met Nancy Toff at an Oxford University Press party, held at the American Historical Association convention 3 years ago. I was not an OUP author, but friends had cajoled me into joining them—if nothing else, they said, the food and drink would be free. I had absolutely no idea what turn my intellectual life was about to take.

Introduced to Ms. Toff, and hearing that she edited children's books, I immediately declared that "we should all be writing for kids. We've gotta get them while they're young. By the time they hit college, it's too late." Enthusiastically, she replied that "if you're serious, why don't you?" A few months later, she invited me to write on Tom Paine as part of a new series of biographies.

Her offer thrilled me. Paine had been my hero ever since childhood, and I knew I'd never get around to writing an adult biography (if for no other reason than that two outstanding works had just appeared by Jack Fruchtmann and John Keane). Truly, Paine's life and writings have always fascinated me. His *Common Sense* turned a colonial rebellion into a revolution; his *American Crisis* inspired the troops and citizenry through hard times; his *Rights of Man* shook the powers of the Atlantic World; his *Age of Reason* offered a brilliant critique of organized religion; and his *Agrarian Justice* foresaw social democracy. That's greatness.

The project excited me all the more because I imagined myself writing for my own daughters, Rhiannon and Fiona, then aged 16 and 12. Indeed, I figured they would serve as my "in-house" editors.

Maybe my generation has begun to develop an interest in writing for young people because we have reached middle age and now have "young adult readers" of our own. But I think it involves more than age and parenthood. While professors have been parenting for generations, they have not been writing for teenagers.

To be honest, along with wanting to write for my kids and their friends, I hoped that the experience would better equip me to pursue the role of "public intellectual." (As one of my campus colleagues sadly observed, the average American reads at about the fifth-grade level, that is, like an 11-year old.) When I admitted as much to Nancy Toff, she proudly recalled that another of her authors had remarked how writing for her was like attending a "boot camp" for public intellectuals.

Though I had always prided myself on writing clearly, I truly had a lot to learn. A smart, appreciative, and critical editor, Nancy would return my chapters having filled the margins with notes flagging where I needed to identify individuals, define terms, clarify references, *and* get rid of jargon. It definitely was not a matter of "dumbing down" the text, or even of simplifying. It had far more to do with explaining things better. Also, Nancy gave me new rules to follow, such as *no* footnotes and *no* quoting of or referring to the work of other historians (other than by way of a bibliography of suggested readings).

I think I learned to tell a better story. Moreover, since such books entail lots of illustrations, I had the fun while writing of making up a wish list of the pictures and maps to accompany the text (not to mention, OUP both assigns someone else the task of securing the preferred illustrations *and* covers the required fees).

My manuscript has now gone into production. Oxford expects to launch the new series this coming year in the fall 2000, and Nancy promises me that *Thomas Paine: Firebrand of the Revolution* will appear among the very first titles. Though there exist innumerable publishers of kids' books, so far Oxford remains the only *university* house to have developed a children's and young adult publishing program. Of course, if Oxford succeeds, other university presses will surely move into the market. And if my OUP colleagues and I are at all representative, I expect many more academics will seek to write such works. I personally assumed I would do it once and move on, but, having learned so much, and having really enjoyed myself in the process, I now keep wondering whom I could write about next.

Chapter 17

ARE AMERICANS MORE INQUISITIVE?

Do Americans ask questions of themselves and their fellow citizens more than do other peoples? I regularly reject discussions of national character (except at dinner parties). But consider the following . . .

Whether it's a consequence of the culture wars, the end of the Cold War, postmodern skepticism, the impending change of millennium, *or* a cultural contribution of the generations of Talmudic-trained Jews who made America home, the USA seems awash in questions.

Walk into any bookstore, you discover innumerable titles like *1001 Questions on [whatever]* and *The Kids Book of Questions on [again, whatever]*. Drive along any boulevard, you see billboards like those of the Dairy Association on which celebrities, upper lips adorned with white mustaches, ask "Got Milk?" Or turn on the television, you find shows like *Jerry Springer* with their guests shouting "Who the **** do you think you are?" Not to mention, Generation X has given way to the (more quizzical?) Generation Y.

Intellectuals, too, have taken to introducing their concerns in queries (remember Francis Fukuyama's "The End of History?"?). Most focus on the state of the nation. On the right, *American Enterprise* kicks off 1999 with "Is America Turning a Corner?: Startling New Trends in Crime, Illegitimacy . . ."; *Insight Magazine*, seeking political consolation after the 1998 elections and Clinton's acquittal, asks "After Three Decades, Has the Conservative Movement Triumphed?"; *Commentary* anxiously poses questions about "Clinton, the Country, and the Public Culture." And renegade radical David Horowitz, apparently eager to revive McCarthyism, publishes silly lists of "Who Is Left?" in *Frontpage Magazine*. Meanwhile, on the left, the editors of *Social Policy* entreat "What's Left?" And, in the country that has made a fetish of surveys and polls, Richard Morin at *The Washington Post* notes how "everybody has an opinion when questions about everyday things are asked."

Originally appeared in *The Times Higher Education Supplement*, May 29, 1999.

On a grander scale, pundits, professors, and theologians nervously ponder America's prospects. Conservative *First Things: A Journal of Religion and Public Life* recently ran the controversial "End of Democracy?" series on morality and the state, which generated so much argument and attention that the editors produced two volumes of articles. And Jim Wallis, Christian Left publisher of *Sojourners*, advances an alternative vision of religion and civil society in *Who Speaks for God?*[1]

In more secular terms, journalists Donald Barlett and James Steele survey America's growing inequality in *America, What Went Wrong?* and *America, Who Stole the Dream?*; sociologist G. William Domhoff provides a new edition of *Who Rules America?*; urban planner Harvey Jacobs asks *Who Owns America?*; journalist William Greider offers a power-structure exposé in *Who Will Tell the People?*; and columnist Eric Alterman addresses democracy and foreign policy in *Who Speaks for America?*[2]

Looking abroad, *World Press Review* devotes an issue to foreign attacks on Uncle Sam titled: "Arrogant? Violent? Bigoted?: Bashing America," and the muckraking *Mother Jones* focuses on "What Happens When America Conquers the Globe?: AMERICA [the brand]."

On an even grander historical (metahistorical?) scale, scholars earnestly inquire into America's "meaning." American exceptionalism tops the charts. Instigating fresh exchanges, Byron Shafer edited *Is America Different?* Yet another Englishman, Graham Wilson—now a Wisconsin professor, married to an American—has recently gotten into the spirit with *Only in America?* And Richard Etulain offers a retrospective anthology on historian Frederick Jackson Turner's thesis, *Does the Frontier Experience Make America Exceptional?* Why not? Our politics inspired German sociologist Werner Sombart to author "Why is there no socialism in the United States?"[3]

Introducing *The Next American Nation*, conservative-turned-liberal Michael Lind recalls a post–Civil War Senate speech to inquire "Are We a Nation?"[4] Writing in the neoconservative policy journal *Public Interest*, Wilfred McClay harkens back to the Founders and asks "Is America an Experiment?" Pragmatist philosopher Richard Rorty organized a conference at the University of Virginia to debate "Does America Have a Democratic Mission?" And, again, given Americans' penchant for the divine, the editors of the centrist *Brookings Review* wonder "What's God Got to Do with the American Experiment?"

Reflecting on multiculturalism, in *The Good Citizen* ethicists David Batstone and Eduardo Mendieta solicit opinions on "What does it mean to be an American?"; and in *Is America Breaking Apart?* social scientists John Hall and Charles Lindholm render a critical yet reassuring Weberian reply.[5]

Given the historical echoes, I wonder if questioning wasn't built right into the very foundations of our "imagined community." In *Letters from an American Farmer* (1782), Jean de Crevecoeur laid the groundwork with: "What, then, is the American, this new man?" And in *The Federalist Papers* (1787), Alexander Hamilton chauvinistically endowed us with a powerful and enduring Enlightenment challenge: "It seems to have been reserved to the people of this country, by their conduct and example, to decide the important question, whether societies of men are really capable or not of establishing good government from reflection and choice, or whether they are forever destined to depend for their political constitutions on accident and force."

I started to imagine an interrogative *History of the United States*, including: abolitionist Sojourner Truth's legendary "Ain't I a Woman?" (1851); laborist Samuel Gompers's "What Does the Working Man Want?" (1890); populist William Jennings Bryan's 1908 campaign motto "Shall the People Rule?"; Depression-era songwriters E. Y. Harburg and Jay Gorney's "Brother, Can You Spare a Dime?" and miner's daughter Florence Reece's "Which Side Are You On?"; the House Un-American Activities Committee's "Are you now or have you ever been a member of the Communist party?"; John Kennedy's "Ask not what your country can do for you—ask what you can do for your country"; folksinger Pete Seeger's "Where Have All the Flowers Gone?" . . .

Reaching into the next century and beyond, this spring *Harper's Magazine* set up a "conversation" between socialist -feminist critic Barbara Ehrenreich and the more conservative anthropologist Lionel Tiger to discuss "Who Needs Men?" And philosopher Gregory Pence considers what strikes me as an unappealing alternative to the missionary position in *Who's Afraid of Human Cloning?*[6]

Amused colleagues, students, and family members eagerly added to my collection of Frequently Asked Questions (FAQs): *MAD* poster-boy Alfred E. Neumann's "What, me worry?"; comedy-team Bud Abbott and Lou Costello's baseball routine, "Who's on first? . . . "; Bugs Bunny's "What's up, doc?"; *Dallas*'s "Who shot J. R.?"; Dion and the Belmonts' "Why Must I Be a Teenager in Love?"; Paul Simon's "Where have you gone, Joe DiMaggio?" . . .

Even our university chancellor unknowingly got into the act when he spoke to the faculty senate on the questions students should be considering: "Who am I? What am I here for? Where am I going?" I would go on, but I have to compose questions for my students' midterm exams. Anyhow, what do you think?

Chapter 18

SEND IN THE HISTORIANS—
OR THE YANKS ARE COMING OVER THERE

To help keep the peace, it looks like we Americans may need to send not only combat troops to Europe but also historians. New conflicts, this time over Europe's past and how it should be publicly represented, seem to demand our intervention.

Early this year, on January 29, 2000, *The New York Times* reported on an official European gathering convened to formulate plans for the creation of a "Museum of Europe," to be constructed in Brussels near the European Parliament. As European Commission President Romano Prodi explained the project: "We are seeking a shared identity—a new European soul.... We need to build a union of hearts and minds, a shared sense of common destiny, of European citizenship."

Nice sentiments. Yet, not surprisingly, the deliberations seem to have gone rather poorly. Talk of *"national* heritage" alone regularly incites competition, contestation, and, often, real rancor. Trying to concoct a *transnational* citizenship, identity, and memory becomes all the more challenging and contentious a task, even in this age of corporate globalism or, as political scientist Benjamin Barber puts it, "McWorld."

For starters, the Greek government has strenuously objected to the museum planners' historical perspective. The Hellenes discovered that, instead of emphasizing Europe's origination of the "democratic idea," the museum's curators-to-be had decided to build the institution's historical narrative around the idea of a "united Europe." As the latter envisioned it, the story should commence not in ancient Greece and the classical world but, rather, in the early Middle Ages with tales of Charlemagne's empire and Latin Christendom.

The story in the *Times* did indicate that several "pan-European" cultural exhibitions were already underway on the continent. However, fully

---

Originally appeared in *The Times Higher Education Supplement*, March 31, 2000.

expecting further fireworks, reporter Michael Wise pointed out that the Italian government had yet to weigh in on the question.

What about you Britons, my English-speaking cousins? Will you simply defer to Gallic ambitions? Wise noted that one British participant in the gathering proposed, with a smile on his face, that the museum procure one of Margaret Thatcher's handbags for exhibition "as a symbol of her angry opposition to taxpayer support for the European Union."

I enjoyed the humor, but is that the best you can do? You could subscribe to *The Economist*'s view of things. The February 12, 2000, cover bluntly asked, "What is Europe?" To which the editors replied within: "Forget geography, forget culture. The thing called 'Europe' . . . is about politics and economics." (Indeed, while we're on the subject, can somebody please tell me what makes Europe a continent?)

Anyhow, before the euro joins the ha'penny in the dustbin of numismatic history, the European Union disintegrates, and xenophobia rears its ugly head beyond the confines of the Balkans and Austria, I want to urge European leaders to seek the renegotiation of the Atlantic Alliance. Rather than merely seeking to stretch its geographical reach eastward, they should petition the U.S. government to enlarge NATO's purview to include cultural affairs. Then they would be entitled to request the stationing of American scholars in Europe, scholars who could effectively cultivate European history, memory, and heritage.

I do not suggest you simply model European history after American history (however often I have heard various statesmen eagerly speak of a "United States of Europe"). That would be foolish, if not impossible. We Yanks, too, currently find ourselves in the midst of rather contentious deliberations about grand narratives, specifically America's own—though, arguably, contentiousness is what the American narrative has been about (weren't we founded in a revolution?).

Nevertheless, I do think you folks could learn about *European* history from us. We've been teaching it for generations. Early in the last century, as part of a broader public campaign to integrate diverse immigrant communities into a common national culture, American historians crafted courses in "Western Civilization" (sometimes now referred to as "From Plato to NATO"). They really rendered a grand history of Europe and the world made by Europeans, culminating in the ascendance of the United States. As UCLA historian Eugen Weber has observed: "French, British, Italian, German historians treat Europe and the wider world as context; Americans treat Europe as text—as 'roots.'"

Larger American universities do offer courses in the respective European national histories, but the foundation courses are almost always organized along pan-European lines. In fact, the teaching of British history has more and more often been incorporated into European "survey classes."

Admittedly, in an increasingly diverse America we have had to rethink the content of "Western Civ." But that just means you Europeans could buy our old textbooks at discounted prices. Of course, I should warn you that the better-written volumes do cover the Spanish Inquisition, the transatlantic slave trade, the establishment of overseas empires, the two world wars, and the Holocaust. But, hey, what's "heritage" without a little blood?

Still, if you think mass murder and exploitation will detract from a "proper" appreciation of European history and heritage, you could restrict your request for American aid to conservative public intellectuals. As we see in Hilton Kramer and Roger Kimball's *The Future of the European Past*,[1] their culture-war campaigns persistently involve condemning the American professorate for failing to revere and transmit the greatness of Western Civilization and Europe's contributions to the making of the modern world.

I can see and hear it now: squadrons of historical scholars, armed with textbooks, singing George M. Cohan's "Over there, over there; Send the word, send the word over there; That the Yanks are coming, the Yanks are coming, the Yanks are coming over there . . ."

Chapter 19

RADICAL AMBIVALENCE

Organized into sections on race, class, war, law, history, and politics, *The Zinn Reader* brings together a selection of 60 articles, essays, speeches, reviews, editorials, and memoirs written in the course of the past 35 years by America's premier radical historian, Howard Zinn.[1] To be honest, I have never felt so ambivalent about a book as I do about this one—indeed, no historian incites in me such mixed feelings as does Zinn.

Zinn is one of America's best-known historians. And, in the best American tradition, he comes from a humble background. He grew up in Depression-era New York, the child of Jewish working-class parents ("Growing Up Class-Conscious"). After laboring in the Brooklyn Navy Yard as a teenager, he served as a bombardier in the Second World War ("The Bombing of Royan") and then attended university on the GI Bill for veterans. He has been both a prolific writer and an energetic activist; as he proudly explains, his scholarship and politics have inspired each other ("The Uses of Scholarship").

Zinn has persistently sought to make history as well as write about it. He first taught at Spelman (1956–63), a Black women's college in Atlanta, where he and his students enlisted in the civil rights movement ("The Southern Mystique" and "Finishing School for Pickets"). In 1963, he moved to Boston University, but he remained active in civil rights campaigns and moved energetically into the anti-war movement ("Vietnam: A Matter of Perspective"). In the course of these struggles, he developed interests in working-class history ("The Ludlow Massacre") and the politics of history and public memory ("Historian as Citizen" and "Columbus and Western Civilization"). In time he would also confront his university's eccentric and conservative president, John Silber ("A University Should Not Be a Democracy").[2]

Scholars traditionally have prided themselves on their objectivity and originality. Zinn has eschewed neither, but he has understood and pursued

---

Originally appeared in *The Times Higher Education Supplement*, March 20, 1998.

them in more critical ways than have most. As the title of one of his books puts it—*You Can't Be Neutral on a Moving Train*[3]—objectivity does not mean refusing to take sides. The critical and democratic scholar must stand with the oppressed and the exploited. Objectivity still means making every effort to recognize where you might be wrong. Yet it also necessarily means making every effort to avoid being taken in by the powerful and trying to see things from the bottom up.

Originality too often has been equated simply with making incremental additions to knowledge on some narrowly defined subject. Zinn has made traditional contributions, for example his award-winning dissertation book, *LaGuardia in Congress*.[4] However, his most original and important contribution has been as a synthesizer and popularizer. His book *A People's History of the United States* has gone into more than 25 printings and sold over 450,000 copies (plus, a new "teaching edition" has been issued by the New Press).[5] Yet, as much of the contents of the present volume attest, another of his major contributions has been his writings as a historical critic.

For these reasons I have greatly admired Howard Zinn. Moreover, I have regularly used his work in my teaching, and I have often quoted him in my writing. So much of *The Zinn Reader* is really valuable. However, I find some of the arguments included in this collection to be irresponsible, if not reprehensible.

Zinn refuses the distinction between "just and unjust wars" and "universally rejects war as a solution to any human problem." He even rejects the justness of the war against Hitler's Germany ("Just and Unjust Wars"). Pacifism on moral grounds I understand, even if I do not agree with it. The late E. P. Thompson's *"historical* pacifism," which distinguished between pre-nuclear and nuclear ages, I understood and appreciated.[6] But Zinn essentially offers us neither. Rather, he attempts to rationalize his universalist and absolutist position on supposedly historical and political grounds by way of examples that are not thought through in either deeply moral or critically historical terms.

Zinn emphasizes that wars rarely—if ever—have been entered into for the ideals proclaimed by the respective leaders. Fair enough. Nevertheless, the cynicism of leaders does not mean that all wars have been wrong and/or futile, *or* that those who did the fighting did so unaware of their leaders' cynicism and ambitions, *or* that they did so without aspirations of their own.

Furthermore, Zinn fails to grant that the worst horrors of war might have been avoided by not having hesitated to go to war in the first place (even though, at times, his own arguments would seem to lead to such a conclusion). In this vein, I find Zinn's discussion of the Second World War and the Holocaust truly outrageous. He states that he does not intend by his words to "remove the responsibility from Hitler and the Nazis." And yet he writes (reminding me of the claims made in recent years by German revisionist historians and, I hope, making the reasons for my revulsion all the more evident): "Not only did waging war against Hitler fail to save the Jews, it may be that the war brought on the Final Solution of genocide . . . Hitler's early aim was forced emigration, not extermination, but the frenzy of [war] created an atmosphere in which the policy turned to genocide."

We should definitely hold British, French, Soviet, and American leaders historically accountable, both for failing to provide refuge for German Jewry and for failing to stand up to Hitler sooner than they did. However, Zinn's remarks imply more than that, leading me to seriously wonder about his historical reasoning.

Chapter 20

REMEMBERING AND HONORING OUR FATHERS—OR DEMOCRATIC GENERATIONS

Decades have been turned into commodities—the '70s, the '60s, and the '50s have all been reified, reduced to fashion, or subsumed to commercial ends. Most recently, it seems to have happened to the 1940s. Swing music has returned to the Top 40 and young people—adorned in "zootsuits and skirts that twirl"—once again jitterbug in nightclubs. The Second World War has returned to the screen in films like *Saving Private Ryan* and *The Thin Red Line*. And books like Tom Brokaw's *The Greatest Generation* and Stephen Ambrose's *Citizen Soldiers* have become bestsellers.[1]

Yet popular interest in the 1940s has to do with more than commerce. Pundits have interpreted it as a matter of "generational politics"—the 1940s *vs.* the 1960s. Conservatives talk about a generation that recognized its patriotic duty compared to one that shirked it. And, sadly, leftists too often defer to such claims, seeing the films and books as attacks on the sixties generation and a means of cultivating support for renewing American militarism.

I, too, usually seek political-economic explanations for cultural developments. But I do not think commerce or politics really explains the current attention to the World War II generation. Undeniably, corporate and party ambitions seek to exploit it. Nevertheless, popular interest emerges from deeper needs and sentiments. Brokaw is right. Those who lived through the Depression of the 1930s, confronted Fascism, and made postwar America are, for all their sins, the "greatest generation." And, as he registers, we are losing them: "The sad reality is that they are dying at an ever faster pace. They're in the mortality years now, in their seventies and eighties, and the Department of Veterans' Affairs estimates that about thirty-two hundred World War II vets die every month."

I readily believe Stephen Spielberg when he says he made the film *Saving Private Ryan* to honor his father, an Army Air Corps radio operator

---

Originally appeared at *TomPaine.com*, January 13, 2000.

on a B-25, and his father's generation.² I share his admiration for our parents' generation.

My own father, Murray Kaye, fought in the Battle of the Bulge as part of General Patton's Third Army. Like so many of his fellow veterans, he rarely spoke of his combat experience. What my mother told me motivated me to regularly badger my dad for details, but he never elaborated, least of all about any heroics on his part. I only knew that a German shell had torn into his tank and, because he happened to be "lucky enough" to be in the gunner's position, shrapnel ripped into his knee, not his head. Wounded in combat, he received the Purple Heart, which my mom, not my dad, showed me. I only got the full story as an adult, and it didn't come directly from him.³

Born in 1923 in Brooklyn, New York, my father had plenty of good reasons to become an angry young man. Yet he didn't, ever. In all the pictures I've seen of him as a youth, he always has the biggest grin of everyone in the photo, a truly great smile, which he never lost. After high school, he entered New York University with the intention of going on to law school (as had my grandfather). However, the war intervened. He tried to enlist in the Navy, but they rejected him for health reasons. Later, the Army drafted him. I don't know if it really happened this way, but my dad used to say that on account of his high IQ scores the Army offered him a choice of officer training or engineering school, and he chose the latter because they told him it would take more time to complete.

Thus, the Army sent him off to Washington State College in Pullman. He never hesitated to talk about his time in eastern Washington. Apparently, he really enjoyed himself. I remember his readily admitting how he had not been a great student, how he studied simply to "pass" (and he never pressured me about grades). Though not a high school athlete, at Washington State he became heavily involved in athletics, playing quarterback on the football team.

Following basic engineering training, the Army transferred him, first to coastal artillery, then to the 42nd Tank Battalion of the 11th Armored Division. Just as in so many movies: Before shipping out to England he asked Frances Sehres (my mom) to marry him. They had known each other since childhood, and my mom swears that when they were only 5 years old he had promised they would one day get married.

In December 1944, the German Army made a last desperate effort to reverse the course of the war. They had been in retreat since D-Day, June 6, 1944. Now, under Hitler's direct orders, three German armies of 500,000 men staged a massive surprise counteroffensive in the Ardennes Forest of Belgium and Luxembourg. The Battle of the Bulge had begun.⁴

Undertrained and inexperienced, the 11th Armored Division was quickly moved from England to the Continent in response to the German advance. And, at the end of December, they were ordered into battle near Bastogne, Belgium. The town is still remembered as the place where totally surrounded American forces refused to surrender to the Germans, the American commander issuing the simple reply "Nuts!"

On January 1, New Year's Day 1945, the 42nd Tank Battalion received specific orders to open a road to Bastogne. Intelligence reported they would face only "enemy infantry with machine guns." But intelligence had it wrong, badly wrong. Having disposed of the infantry, the 42nd, in their light tanks, ran head on into a farm field filled with the far more substantial German Tiger tanks outfitted with their infamous 88-millimeter guns.

Though the 42nd would eventually secure their objective, their losses would be very heavy. A German tank cannon scored a direct hit on my father's tank. My father, his left leg badly wounded, reached down and grabbed his sergeant. Somehow he managed to get himself and the sergeant up and out of the tank and onto the ground. With only one leg able to bear weight, my father slung the man over his shoulder and started "running" for cover while German machine guns raked the snow-covered ground. My father said he knew he was hit in the leg but was too frightened to look at it.

My father's company commander, Eli Warach, rushed over and leapt out of his own tank to help. Warach recalled how my father, with a bone of his leg sticking out of his pants, responded by shouting at him: "You schmuck, get out of here. You'll get killed." But Warach ignored the remark, boosted my dad and the sergeant onto the back of his tank, and took them to a medical station. The sergeant died. My father was fortunate. He had a "million-dollar wound"—not so bad as to disable him, but severe enough to send him home. There he recovered, married my mom, and worked hard to secure a good life for his family.

Stephen Ambrose says the "GIs fought because they had to. What held them together was not country and flag, but unit cohesion." And yet, he grants there is more to be said. The GIs "were the children of democracy and they did more to help spread democracy around the world than any other generation in history. At the core, the American citizen soldiers knew the difference between right and wrong, and they didn't want to live in a world in which wrong prevailed. So they fought, and won, and we all of us living and yet to be born, must be forever grateful."

My generation is not that of my father's. We confronted different histories. Yet we are our parents' children. And that is how we should start thinking about the sixties generation. Contrary to those who insist on a great divide between the 1940s and the 1960s, I see great continuity. Both those of us who entered the service during the Vietnam War and those of us who did not felt we knew the difference between right and wrong and what it took to honor democratic life. Like our parents, we didn't want to live in a world in which wrong prevailed. My father grasped that. And when, in 1968, I told him that I would not allow myself to be drafted—not as a pacifist, but as an opponent of an un-American, illegal, and immoral war—he said he understood and supported my decision. His was truly the greatest generation.

Chapter 21

FANNING THE SPARK OF HOPE IN THE PAST: THE BRITISH MARXIST HISTORIANS

We have assembled to assess twentieth-century historiographies. And I shall speak of the British Marxist historians. But, first, I would ask: How should we pursue such assessments? Beyond the essential scholarly objectivity, and the desired literary artistry, what should we value in the writing of history?

We could defer to ascendant forces. Acknowledging the triumph of capital, we could rank historiographical traditions in terms of the total sales figures of their scholars' books. Or, in view of resurgent fundamentalisms, we could base our assessments on how often state and priestly authorities have included a particular school's writings in official canons and curricula.

Of course, I joke. And yet, given the respective imperatives of capitalism and fundamentalism, I do so with some anxiety. Still, how should we assay twentieth-century historiographies?

Because our answers will surely reflect our differing conceptions of the purpose and promise of historical study and thought, I'll start by making clear my own.

Like so many of my generation, I entered historical studies possessed of a vision of the discipline in which we were to serve as citizen-scholars, contributing to ongoing struggles for liberty, equality, and democracy by cultivating critical historical memory, consciousness, and imagination.

Undeniably, circumstances have changed. We have aged. The struggles have abated. Nevertheless, the challenges and responsibilities persist. Arguably, they have become all the greater.

French historian François Furet closed his recent history of twentieth-century Communism, *The Passing of an Illusion*, with reflections on the state of politics and political vision. To his credit, Furet—who in his youth had

---

Originally presented in a longer version as a plenary address at the international congress "History Under Debate," held in Santiago de Compostela, Galicia, Spain, July 14–18, 1999, and appeared in *Rethinking History*, vol. 4, no. 3, 2000.

stood on the left, but after 1956 moved steadily rightward—did not accept that humanity was incapable of imagining and pursuing anything more progressive than *capitalist* democracy. He did not subscribe to Francis Fukuyama's thesis about the "end of history" or Margaret Thatcher's assertion, parroted today by politicians right *and* left, that "there is no alternative." Furet wrote:

> The idea of *another* society has become almost impossible to conceive of, and no one in the world today is offering any advice on the subject or even trying to formulate a new concept. Here we are, condemned to live in the world as it is. This condition is too austere and contrary to the spirit of modern societies to last. Democracy, by virtue of its existence, creates the need for a world beyond the bourgeoisie and beyond Capital, a world in which a genuine human community can flourish. . . . The proletarian revolution, Marxist-Leninist science, the ideological election of a party, a territory, or an empire have undoubtedly come to an end along with the Soviet Union. The disappearance of these figures familiar to our century brings our age to a close; it does not, however, spell the end of the democratic repertory.[1]

Of course, historians cannot themselves conjure up a political vision for the twenty-first century, democratic or otherwise. However, we do have much to offer to democratic thought and politics.

Ruling classes rightly fear history and persistently try to control knowledge and understanding of the past in hopes of persuading those whom they dominate that the way things are is the way they ought to be—or, at least, the only way they can be.

Wielding the powers of the past, historians can encourage awareness that, however tragic and ironic the dialectic of history, the creation of polities and social orders characterized by greater freedom, equality, and democracy remains possible. Furthermore, we can advance the *historical* education of desire, informing popular deliberations and agencies with the experiences, aspirations, and visions of those who have preceded us.[2]

The words of the German-Jewish critic, Walter Benjamin, continue to summon us: "Only that historian will have the gift of fanning the spark of hope in the past who is firmly convinced that *even the dead* will not be safe from the enemy [the ruling class] if he wins. And the enemy has not ceased to be victorious."[3]

I now turn to speak of the British Marxist historians. I refer specifically to the "generation" that included senior figures like Cambridge University economist Maurice Dobb and journalists and writers A. L. Morton and Dona Torr but whose central and foremost members were Rodney Hilton,

Christopher Hill, George Rudé, (E. P.) Edward Thompson, Dorothy Thompson, John Saville, Eric Hobsbawm, and Victor Kiernan.[4]

The intellectual and political formation of this generation began in the 1930s, in the shadows of the Depression, the triumph of Fascism in Central and Southern Europe, and the ever-increasing likelihood of a second world war. Perceiving the British Labour party as incapable of adequately addressing the crisis of capital and the threat to freedom and democracy, those then-young men and women joined the Communist party while at university, hoping to contribute to working-class struggles and the making of socialism.

Following the war, during which many of them served in the British Army, they came together in the Communist Party Historians' Group, eager to foster and popularize a Marxist interpretation of English and British history. Though their collective endeavors met with limited success beyond Marxist circles, one initiative, pursued independently by several Group members, led to the founding of the now-prestigious journal *Past & Present* (1952).

Of far greater import, the Group served as the incubator of British Marxist historiography. Here, we should not fail to appreciate the contributions of Dobb, Torr, and Morton. In *Studies in the Development of Capitalism*, Dobb provided the Group's original historiographical problematic and framework (the transition from feudalism to capitalism); directed members' thinking away from economic and technological determinisms, toward a richer political-economic analysis; and focused their historical attentions on class relations and conflicts.[5]

Drawing on the radical labor-history tradition cultivated by Sydney and Beatrice Webb, John and Barbara Hammond, and G. D. H. Cole,[6] Morton and Torr impressed upon their younger colleagues that the refashioning of British history must entail more than emphasizing political economy and class. It must involve, as well, the recovery of the experiences of the "common people." In *A People's History of England*, Morton led the way in "democratizing" the past by extending the bounds of *who* was to be included in the historical record and by making that record accessible to a popular readership.[7] And Torr, though she often defended orthodoxy, fervently challenged her comrades to reject economic determinism and fatalism, and seek to understand consciousness and agency in the making of history, especially the consciousness and agency of the "lower orders."[8]

In 1956—in the wake of Khruschev's speech on Stalinism to the Soviet Communist party, the Soviet invasion of Hungary, and the failure of the British Communist party to oppose the invasion and democratize itself—

the majority of the historians resigned from the party in protest (having played leading roles in failed attempts to reform it).

Departing the party and the Group, the historians did not reject socialism, though they now championed a more democratic and humanistic socialist politics. Neither did they abandon Marxism, though they now articulated an even more critical and historical understanding of it.[9] Only the editorial board of *Past & Present* continued to bind them together organizationally after 1956, and yet the histories they wrote register how closely aligned intellectually they remained.

Imbued with the ideas and aspirations engendered in the Group, the younger historians authored their most important works in the decades following the mid-1950s. They didn't just render major contributions to their respective fields of study; they also effectively recast those fields. Consider the work of Rodney Hilton in medieval and peasant studies; Christopher Hill in studies of the seventeenth century and the English Revolution (now often referred to as "Hill's Century"); George Rudé, Eric Hobsbawm, and Edward Thompson in the social history of the Age of Revolution and popular movements; John Saville, Dorothy Thompson, Edward Thompson, and Hobsbawm in the field of nineteenth-century labor history; and Victor Kiernan and Hobsbawm in studies of European history and imperialism.[10]

And, transcending their many individual contributions, the historians "together" made four paramount contributions to historical studies and thought.

First, against the prevailing liberal and Marxist orthodoxies alike, the historians developed class-struggle analysis and demonstrated the class-structured character of history. They drew their central working hypothesis—"The history of all hitherto existing society is the history of class struggle"—from Marx and Engels's *Communist Manifesto* and proceeded, as Marx himself had insisted, to study history afresh. Thus they showed that: The medieval world was not agreeably organized into three estates but, rather, an order of struggle between lords and peasants; the conflicts of seventeenth-century England represented not simply a civil war but, all the more, a "bourgeois revolution" propelled, in part, by struggles of the lower orders; the eighteenth century was not conflict-free but shot through with tensions and antagonisms between "patricians and plebeians" ("class struggle without class," as E. P. Thompson contended); and the Industrial Revolution entailed not only dramatic economic change and social disruption but also, in the course of the battles between "capital and labor," a radical, if not heroic, process of class formation determined in great part by the creative agency of working people themselves.[11]

The historians developed class-struggle analysis not merely to better grasp rebellion and revolution. They also sought to reveal the forms that such struggles took in times of relative social tranquility. They enlarged the very scope of what we should understand as "struggle" and afforded us a fuller appreciation of "resistance" to exploitation and oppression.

Second, the historians critically advanced history from below—or, as we Americans say, "history from the bottom up." The French *Annalistes* may have originated this approach; but the British Marxists turned it in a more critical direction. Given their interest in class struggle, the British Marxists did not fail to attend to the powerful and propertied,[12] but they especially committed their energies to reappropriating the lives and agencies of the laboring classes—peasants, artisans, and workers. In words we have come to know by heart, E. P. Thompson declared his and his comrades' historical ambitions: "I am seeking to rescue the poor stockinger, the Luddite cropper, the 'obsolete' handloom weavers, the utopian artisan, and even the deluded followers of Joanna Southcott from the enormous condescension of posterity."[13]

Third, the historians recovered England's "radical-democratic tradition." They revealed not a narrow history of ideas originating in the heads of intellectuals, but a history of popular ideology standing in dialectical relationship to the traditional history of politics and idea. Now, alongside Magna Carta, we encounter the Peasant Rising of 1381 calling for an end to overlords; outside of Parliament in the seventeenth century, we witness Levellers, Diggers, and Ranters demanding rights and equalities; in the streets of eighteenth-century London, we hear not just John Wilkes but also the crowds of London asserting the "rights of freeborn Englishmen"; and in the Age of Revolution we behold English Jacobins, Luddites, and Chartists planting new trees of liberty and cultivating democratic possibilities.

At the same time, the British Marxists established their own "intellectual" pantheon: John Ball and his fellow radical priests in the late fourteenth century; Gerrard Winstanley, John Milton, and John Bunyan in the seventeenth; John Wilkes, Tom Paine, and Mary Wollstonecraft in the late eighteenth; and William Wordsworth, William Blake, William Cobbett, Robert Owen, Ernest Jones, Karl Marx, and William Morris in the nineteenth.[14]

Finally, by way of class-struggle analysis, history from the bottom up, and the recovery of the radical-democratic tradition, the British Marxists effectively "deconstructed" the grand narratives of right *and* left. They undermined the unilinear, Liberal–Whig and orthodox–marxist versions of history in which, in the former case, modern English freedoms are comprehended as the outcome of a continuously unfolding, ever-advancing, evolutionary process commencing in Anglo-Saxon times and, in the latter, world history is conceived of as a prearranged series of progressive stages determined by technological and economic developments. And they challenged the Cold War modernizationist and Cold War Marxist stories of the making of the modern world, both of which accentuated and celebrated the "role of the bourgeoisie and middle classes" in the development of capitalism *and* liberal democracy.

The British Marxists confronted the myths of postwar social science and history, such as "peasant passivity" and "working-class authoritarianism," and they excavated and laid the foundations for a new grand narrative. This new narrative appreciates human agency and the fundamental role of working people in the making of the modern world, not just as laborers and material providers but also as progenitors of and aspirants for freedom, equality, and democracy. Dreams of proletarian revolution aside, we now know that the "working class has proved to be—with few exceptions— the most consistently pro-democratic social class."[15]

Stated in the briefest terms: The British Marxist historical tradition has influenced work across the social sciences and humanities, from labor, slavery, and peasant studies to literary, cultural, and women's studies. And their own works—so very English in character—have inspired critical scholarship globally.

Admittedly, in the years following 1956, political participation and activism varied among the historians. But every one of them remained committed to recovering the past from the bottom up, making it available beyond the realm of academe, and addressing extra-academic audiences with the historical insights and perspectives secured in the archives. Essays and reviews by Hilton, Hill, Hobsbawm, Thompson, and Kiernan regularly appeared in the periodical press's literary and opinion pages. Though their scholarly accomplishments brought them public prominence, their prominence did not constrain them.[16]

In fact, the British Marxist historians served as an important bridge between the older and newer British lefts. In 1956, John Saville and Edward Thompson published *The Reasoner* to pressure for Communist party reform. On their departure from the party they renamed it *The New Reasoner: A Journal of Socialist Humanism*, and their contributors included their historian comrades and other sympathetic socialists. And, in 1959, they merged *The New Reasoner* with the *Universities and Left Review*, a journal produced by Oxford University students, to create *New Left Review*.[17]

Notably, the two figures of the Group who achieved the greatest scholarly renown, Eric Hobsbawm and Edward Thompson, also came to be recognized as Britain's foremost "public intellectuals" of the left. Hobsbawm had remained in the party, but it did not prevent him from producing great, if not paradigm-setting, work. Indeed, in *The Age of Revolution, 1789–1848*,

The Age of Capital, 1848–1875, *The Age of Empire, 1875–1914*, and *The Age of Extremes, 1914–1991*, he essentially established the temporal framework for the study of modern European and world history.[18] By the late 1970s, Hobsbawm had emerged not only as our "premier Marxist historian" but also as a venerated voice of the British left and (though still a Communist) an adviser to leaders of the Labour party.[19]

Edward Thompson consistently remained the most politically engaged of the historians right up until his early death in 1993. In the tradition of Tom Paine and William Cobbett, he wrote and campaigned for the "rights of freeborn Britons." In the 1950s, he enlisted in the Campaign for Nuclear Disarmament (CND); in the 1970s, he directed brilliant broadsides against the British Establishment, accusing the powers that be of trampling on the rights of British citizens and the social and economic gains they had secured; and, in the early 1980s, he co-founded European Nuclear Disarmament (END). In every instance—whether challenging the structures and agents of the Cold War or those of ruling-class domination—he sought to draw his fellow Britons "out of apathy" by reminding them of their radical heritage.[20]

Perhaps, given the record of our Age of Extremes, modesty, skepticism, and reservation are in order. Yet we do not seem to suffer from democratic audacity, ambition, and hyperactivity but, rather, from amnesia, anomie, and paralysis.

Still, like Furet, I don't believe we've seen the end of history. Democratic aspirations have retreated, but they persist and promise to reassert themselves. For those of us committed to democratic possibilities, our task remains that of advancing the historical education of desire, of cultivating and encouraging critical historical memory, consciousness, and imagination.

Clearly, we have to study the past afresh and write our own histories. We have to develop fresh means of engaging our fellow citizens. And yet, as we confront the powers, mystifications, and illusions of the day, we would do well to appreciate, if not emulate, the work of the British Marxist historians, for they possessed the gift of which Benjamin wrote. They redeemed the lives and struggles of those whose place in the making of history had been neglected or denied. They revealed the ideas and aspirations that motivated the diverse movements of the exploited and oppressed. They contested, and helped to transform, the reigning narratives of past and present. And, doing so, they fanned the spark of hope.

Affairs Academic

Chapter 22

ARE WE GOOD CITIZENS?

In the shadows of the German occupation, Marc Bloch (1886–1944), the greatest of medievalists and co-founder of the *Annales* school of history, posed the essential question for democratic intellectuals, a question that we academics should pose to ourselves in every generation.

In *Strange Defeat* (written in 1940, but published after the Liberation), Bloch recounted his reenlistment in the French army, his subsequent evacuation to England, and his decision to return to France, to his family, *and* to fight again. In particular he examined the developments leading to his country's political and military debacle; however, he did not fail to consider the actions of scholars and academics in the prewar years. These reflections led him to state, near the close of the text: "The real trouble with us professors was that we were absorbed in our day-to-day tasks. Most of us can say with some justice that we were good workmen. Is it equally true to say that we were good citizens?" (Bloch went on to join the Resistance but, tragically, in 1944 he was captured and executed by the Gestapo.)[1]

In the face of class, racial, and gender oppressions, and the devastation of both the Cold War and a murderous war in Southeast Asia, just such a question informed the thinking of my own student generation in the 1960s and early 1970s. I am sure that those of us who took up academic careers had something like it on our minds. Indeed, many of us imagined ourselves becoming *citizen-scholars*, critically transforming, in directions ever more liberal, egalitarian, and democratic, both our academic disciplines and, as public intellectuals, the political and social orders of the day. Political scientist Benjamin Barber expressed our pedagogical philosophy best when he said that "all education is or ought to be radical—a reminder of the past, a challenge to the present, and a prod to the future."

Arguably, in certain fields we have accomplished a great deal. Now middle-aged, we have written libraries of work incorporating the experiences and perspectives of peoples previously excluded from traditional

---

Originally appeared in *The Times Higher Education Supplement*, November 4, 1994.

academic discourse. Further, in addition to carrying out significant changes in our respective disciplines, we have created new ones such as cultural, development, and environmental studies, which treat contemporary issues in original ways.

Nevertheless, we must still ask ourselves if we have been, in Bloch's words, "good citizens." In fact, figures on both the left and the right have accused us of not being so. And, unfortunately, we too often have responded defensively when we should have seriously considered the charges leveled against us. It's not simply a matter of chastising ourselves if we have not been living up to our ideals. Neither should it be for the sake of fabricating rationalizations for where we may have gone astray. Rather, we should do so in order to figure out what we need to do in order to actually realize our aspirations.

In *The Last Intellectuals* and *Dogmatic Wisdom*, Russell Jacoby, one of our own comrades, declaims that we have forsaken the role of citizen-scholars. He charges that we have enclosed ourselves within our campuses and abandoned our promise, or threat, of seeking to transform American politics and society more broadly, expending our efforts instead on professional matters and advancement.[2]

Although Jacoby fails to consider the way in which the corporate-dominated media has collaborated in shifting the political "center" to the right and in marginalizing the intellectual and academic left in public debate, he has issued a serious charge, one that still needs to be properly addressed. We do need urgently to develop new means by which we can better engage and cultivate "publics," as C. Wright Mills put it back on the eve of the unexpected and tumultuous 1960s.[3]

By definition my generation's radical-democratic commitments make us anything but good citizens to political conservatives, and to listen to them you would believe we had nearly achieved our wildest dreams and their worst nightmares. They have pursued their corporately funded campaigns against us in terms of "the crisis of history," "the battle of the books," "the collapse of the canon," "PC wars," and "the dangers of multiculturalism." New Right figures, like Irving Kristol, William Bennett, Dinesh D'Souza, Martin Anderson, and Lynn Cheney, would practically have us indicted as traitors for our work as teachers and writers. They claim we have been subverting the nation from our privileged sanctuaries in colleges and universities.

They assert that as "tenured radicals" we have been turning out graduates who are ill- and/or misinformed about capitalism and the Western heritage and, more seriously, downright hostile toward them. True citizen-scholars, they insist, would not criticize and deconstruct the history and culture of America and the West but rather transmit them and cultivate their appreciation; if we really wanted to act as "good citizens," they argue, we would celebrate America, not cultivate dissent. Moreover, they contend that in our "lust for power" we "socialists, feminists, and multiculturalists" have sought to fashion younger generations in our own images.

To be clear about it, the New Right's attacks have repeatedly misrepresented our aspirations and practices. Commanding media attention, they have construed our efforts at educating students to critical modes of analysis and thought as processes of "indoctrination and propagandizing" and, to cite only the latest of their distortions, they have wrongly, yet deliberately, equated multiculturalism with separatist ideologies like "Afrocentrism."

I could debate the right's limiting notions of what a liberal education ought to entail and of how democratic life is supposed to be lived (as I have done elsewhere). But what concerns me as a teacher is that my generation isn't nearly as successful in cultivating critical radical-democratic intellects as the New Rightists, in however distorted a fashion, think (or, at least, proclaim). Mostly, I worry and grow anxious about the apparent cynicism of contemporary students, their lack of interest in politics and public affairs, and their resignation and deference to the existing political and social order.

I am even led to wonder to what extent our own stories and analyses contribute to the spreading cynicism. Do we talk so much about oppression and exploitation that we fail to recount and value the changes actually wrought by popular democratic struggles? Do we end up dampening or suppressing hope, optimism, and a sense of possibility? A few years ago, one of my students revealed in her final essay that the more aware she becomes of the tragic and ironic character of history, and of the persistence of structures of power and inequality, the less capable she feels of doing anything about them—and the more inclined she becomes to seek merely personal advantage and advancement.

In other words, it appears quite possible that, contrary to our best democratic intentions, my colleagues and I actually have tempered, or even undone, the "innate" progressive inclinations of our students. And, thereby, we have furthered popular acceptance of the idea advanced by the right that we have reached "the end of history," in other words, that we can develop democracy no further.

My colleagues and I should reflect seriously about the narratives of past and present and the understandings of human agency that we offer. Apparently, we need to better communicate that however tragic and ironic modern experience has been, it has also witnessed real progress. That is, however much history has entailed humanly created hells, it has also involved humanly created freedom, equality, and justice.

If my generation is ever truly to be able to answer Bloch's question in the affirmative, we will not only have to redeem our original vision of ourselves as citizen-scholars; we will have to articulate new ways of securing it.

Chapter 23

A NATION OF TEACHERS

Talk about education inevitably incites disagreement and debate. But one statement I make consistently generates approval and consensus: "I never really know something until I have had to teach it to others." Perhaps this simple observation—that teaching enables not just learning, but also knowing—can serve as the starting place for a revolution in education and, even, in public life more broadly.

Most immediately, it involves radically redefining undergraduate education not simply as another level of learning but also as preparation for teaching. That is, we should conceive of all students as future teachers, not only those studying for degrees and certificates in education. Moreover, their undergraduate studies should cultivate pedagogical skills and talents. Grandly speaking, it means creating *a nation of teachers*.

American education has been under siege for most of my adult life. Seeking a scapegoat for everything from economic crisis and decline to the enervation and degeneration of public life and culture, every level and aspect of schooling has come under assault. As the title of a 1983 Department of Education report registers, America is perceived to be *A Nation at Risk*. Not surprisingly, in view of the fundamental role they play in the educational process, teachers have become prime targets of attack, and, along with them, their labor unions and the university schools of education that prepare them.

Grounded in their respective understandings of the contemporary American crisis *and* the purpose and promise of education, critics from right to left have proposed intriguing projects to reform the present system of teacher training. Conservatives are convinced that liberals—no, make that *radicals*—with the massive organizational support of the National Education Association, have controlled America's schools of education for at least a generation. Rita Kramer in *Ed School Follies* and Chester Finn in *We Must Take Charge* have lambasted "ed schools" for their supposedly vapid, if not

---

Originally appeared in *The Times Higher Education Supplement*, March 31, 1995.

silly, curricula and for promoting social causes more than intellectual excellence. And they have gone on to offer a variety of alternative schemes for preparing teachers.[1]

Conservatives defend the idea of teachers as "transmitters" of skills and the nation's cultural heritage. Their plans for teacher training usually involve reducing the number of courses required in education and pedagogy in favor of requiring additional preparation in, respectively, the core disciplines for prospective primary teachers and a particular discipline for prospective high school teachers. Thereafter, prospective teachers would serve a period in classroom apprenticeships under the guidance and assessment of officially recognized "master teachers." In fact, there are some conservatives who would completely eliminate education and pedagogy requirements. They would abolish schools of education altogether and leave questions of educational research and design to the social sciences. (And I cannot deny that many arts and science faculty, who have long been suspicious of teacher education programs, find this idea most appealing.)

Left education critics essentially agree with the conservatives about the staleness and foolishness of ed-school curricula, but they see the problems of education and teacher preparation quite differently. They contend that the nation's schools function merely to reproduce the inequalities and oppressions of industrial-capitalist society. Critical theorists, most notably Henry Giroux in *Schooling and the Struggle for Public Life* and Joe Kincheloe in *Toward a Critical Politics of Teacher Thinking*, have called for the liberation and reconstruction of education. They suggest that we begin by seeing teachers as "transformative intellectuals" rather than merely as "transmitters" of knowledge and skills. Thus, in their view, we need to drastically revise ed-school curricula to incorporate and emphasize historical, political, and multicultural studies—thereby "empowering" teachers to serve as democratic social-change agents capable of developing students as "critical citizens."[2]

Unfortunately, however original, critical, and welcome these proposals seem, they actually are all—both left and right—limited in their vision and imagination. They fail to recognize the truly radical promise and possibility at the heart of teacher education and how we might yet redeem and realize that promise and possibility on a grander scale.

Rather than merely reform or even, more dramatically, abolish teacher education, I would argue that we should convert *all* university and further education into the preparation of teachers. We should conceive of public life in educational terms and appreciate that pedagogical skills are essential to civic and working life. (And let me be absolutely clear about it: I do not suggest this as a way of "discovering" hidden talent, though it could be; nor, for that matter, do I intend it to serve, in political-economic terms, as a means of union-busting by increasing the reserve army of pedagogical labor.)

Conservatives rightly stress the transmission of knowledge and skills. Modern industry and a democratic polity demand a highly skilled and knowledgeable citizenry. To be honest about it, teacher education programs have slighted the primary acquisition of "knowledge" in favor of "method." Not only do standards need to be raised; further and better preparation in the academic disciplines is also imperative.

At the same time, leftists rightly demand progressive changes. Teachers are inherently "intellectuals" (indeed, understood developmentally, so, too, are their students). And if we really want to begin to address America's economic, political, and cultural crises, then we must fully prepare teachers to develop knowledgeable *and* critical citizens and workers. At the least, therefore, we should reform teacher education to accomplish those things. The Italian Marxist Antonio Gramsci stated it smartly: "Democracy, by definition, cannot mean merely that an unskilled worker can become skilled. It must mean that every 'citizen' can 'govern' and that society places him, even if only abstractly, in a general condition to achieve this." Hopefully, both left and right would subscribe to such a vision.

Yet why should we conceive of the transmission of knowledge and the making of critical citizens as activities necessarily limited to the formal education of the young, that is, to primary and secondary schooling? In a modern democracy, shouldn't they be central and ongoing experiences of people throughout the course of their lives both as citizens and workers? Continuing in this vein, why should the capacities, sensibilities, and skills essential to those endeavors be limited to schoolteachers? In a democracy, shouldn't they be developed in all the people? In other words, if we truly seek to advance and enhance both economic development and democratic development, the debate about teacher training must, for a start, include higher and further education generally.

I do not recommend that we merely extend ed-school instruction to all liberal and technical arts programs. Again, we need to seriously revamp ed-school curricula and practices (though outright abolition would be foolish, for surely we will continue to want teachers specially attuned to the particular needs and requirements of children and young people). Furthermore, different circumstances require different pedagogies.

What I do call for, however, is consideration of both the way we currently train teachers for primary and secondary schools *and* the way we educate all our students for public life.

In other words, we should begin to ask how we might better prepare our students to work as "citizen-pedagogues" in the diverse public arenas in which they will be engaged. Clearly, not everyone should be a classroom instructor, but everyone should be capable of practicing the arts of teaching.

POSTSCRIPT

Several developments have led me to return anew to the idea I presented in this particular chapter. And I have become all the more convinced that we should cultivate student skills and knowledge through a program of "learning through teaching," especially if we want to prepare and encourage students to become smart, articulate, and engaged citizens and professional practitioners.

Growing concern about the state of American civil society and public life has instigated continuing discussion in higher education about what colleges and universities might do to cultivate the skills and sensibilities of good citizenship. Most notably, schools across the country have instituted community service requirements for their undergraduates. I appreciate such endeavors; however, I think that too often we reduce good citizenship to "doing good and charitable works."

Given the prevailing and intensifying structure of inequality and power—and the impact it has on life in America—good citizenship would seem to demand not only learning to do good deeds but also learning how to connect with one's fellow citizens to confront and challenge power and authority. We should educate our students to *critical* citizenship and afford them the essential knowledge and requisite skills of reading, writing, speaking, and calculation. As I have argued elsewhere, we need to prepare the next generation of public intellectuals.

I have read of a new curricular movement called "speaking across the curriculum," modeled after the 1980s "writing across the curriculum" movement.[3] Activists in the latter contended that to address apparently declining writing skills, colleges and universities needed to rethink how *and* where they taught writing and composition. That is, writing needed to be taught in more than "College Writing" or "English Composition" classes. It needed to be taught in all courses.

We now hear that speaking skills have declined as well and that we should address the problem not merely by requiring public-speaking classes, but all the more by requiring oral exercises in all our classes. I have even come upon articles, like Gary Smith's "Learning to Speak and Speaking to Learn," that directly linked my own conception of learning through teaching to the speaking-across-the-curriculum movement.[4]

Indeed, in January 1999 a very brief story appeared in the London *Times Higher Education Supplement* (where my own column first appeared), leading me to imagine that some folks in British educational policy circles had been persuaded by my argument. Titled "Students Should All Learn to Be Teachers," it simply reported that the Teacher Training Agency was considering a government proposal that all university students "learn to be teachers." No real details were provided. I asked my editor at the paper whether he knew if my column had played into the policy thinking. He happily replied—no doubt both to make me feel good and to register the influence of the paper—that, of course, such people follow the paper and garner fresh ideas from its pages.

In any case, I do sense a movement in favor of "learning through teaching." At my own university—where we have a tradition of academic innovation and experimentation—we recently have begun to consider and elaborate original ways by which we might reinvigorate academic life. And the idea has generated a good deal of interest and discussion (see the following chapter and postscript).

In preparation for those deliberations, I reread *The Reconstruction of an American College* (1968), a set of proposals advanced by the great teacher and historian Warren Susman intended to modernize and reinvigorate academic life and learning at Rutgers College (then an all-male institution), where I was then an undergraduate. It both humbled and excited me to rediscover his words: "An educated man is one who can transfer his awareness and understanding to others, can use his skill in some larger social contexts. One truly knows when he is able to interpret what he knows to others. Thus, a true college would be a community of scholars and of teachers, with all of us, faculty and students, operating as both."

Chapter 24

STARTING ALL OVER AGAIN

I am a chauvinist regarding my academic home, the University of Wisconsin–Green Bay (UWGB), and, in spite of the nasty budget cuts we are suffering, the thirtieth anniversary of its creation in 1965 by the state legislature provides good reason to celebrate. We have an especially beautiful campus along the bay shore just outside the city, students clamor to be admitted, *and* the special "interdisciplinary and problem-focused" mission of the institution survives, battered yet intact.

UWGB was born of a radical vision. Our contemporary American counterparts include the University of California–Santa Cruz, Washington's Evergreen College, and, in Britain, the universities of Sussex and East Anglia. But the best historical comparison is to University College London (UCL), established in the 1820s, the very first college of the University of London. Like UCL in its time, we were all established to offer an alternative to the conservatism of existing (and far older) institutions by providing degrees more engaging of the rhythms and problems of modern life. (UCL, in stark contrast to the "ancient" universities at Oxford and Cambridge, admitted women, did not restrict admission to members of the Church of England, and offered degrees in modern liberal arts subjects and medicine.)

Indeed, because his commitment to the foundation and continuing success of UWGB always reminded me of the philosopher Jeremy Bentham's to UCL, I suggested to our now-retired first chancellor, Edward Weidner, that he emulate Bentham's "auto-iconic" presence at UCL. With affection and a smile, I proposed to Weidner that he will his body to the Human Biology program for use as a cadaver, on condition the university promises to cover his skeleton in a plaster-cast likeness and situate it in a glass-fronted booth at the main entrance. Encouragingly, I told him how, as a graduate student in London, I felt I owed it to Bentham to wish "good day" to his mannequin every time I entered the UCL campus.

Originally appeared in *The Times Higher Education Supplement*, September 8, 1995. The postscript originally appeared as a World View column, "Travails of the Trailblazers," *The Times Higher Education Supplement*, December 17, 1999.

UWGB stood in the vanguard of the 1960s movement to transform higher education. Our very academic organization turned the world upside down by making interdisciplinary programs the primary budgetary and teaching units and subordinating the traditional disciplines to them. Moreover, although dullards, faint-hearts, and reactionaries have occasionally tried to restore the traditional order, the interdisciplinary departments—like Communications and the Arts, Humanistic Studies, Urban Studies, and Human Development—remain at the core. (Naturally, there are some funny stories about the names first given to the newly conceived departments. One had the bizarre title "Analysis Synthesis" and was assigned the official acronym "Anal Syn"—which students quickly used to shock their parents.)

Universitywide, my colleagues are a most impressive bunch. To be honest, when I arrived in 1978, a mere 28-year-old, I found their zealous commitment to the mission and progress of the institution not only inspiring but also, on occasion, frightening. And that commitment persists even as the aging process takes its toll.

Just consider that in my first year here there were 150 faculty for 2500 students; today, the same number of faculty are responsible for 4500 students! Furthermore, we are each regularly assessed in the areas of teaching, scholarship, institutional development, and community service. The workload is clearly out of control, but we take some consolation in believing that the late Progressive politician and state governor, "Fightin' Bob" La Follette, would be happy that his "Wisconsin Idea" of a democratic and public service–oriented university is alive and well, at least on our campus.

The students, too, are rather remarkable. At the outset, quite a few were drawn from across the nation by our alternative structure and environmental mission. That has changed. Now, they tend to be overwhelmingly from Wisconsin. What brings them here rather than to another of the campuses of the UW system? I'd like to think it was our curricula, but I must admit that when I ask incoming students, their most popular—and truly American—reply is that UWGB is the only campus in the state whose residence-hall rooms have *private* toilets and baths.

Today's students may seem less involved intellectually (probably a sign of the times more than anything else), but they are no less bright—they might even be smarter—and, in a way that I truly appreciate, they are soundly democratic in their bearing; that is, they respect but do not readily defer to authority. I should add that most come from lower-middle- and working-class backgrounds and are imbued with a solid work ethic; even during the academic year, the majority of them work 20-hour-a-week jobs to pay for their education.

Significantly, the student body has always been composed of a relatively high number of students over the age of 25 (sometimes, well over). Referred to as "nontraditionals," they are actually redeeming and giving new meaning to the great American tradition of self-improvement and the equally American practice of "pickin' up and startin' all over again." They are a diverse lot, but they all bring ideas and experiences from which we have something to learn. Their presence also demands that faculty develop a certain patience and accept that students may well be absent because their children or an elderly parent are sick or, when no babysitters are available, that they'll bring their kids to class.

I have always felt a special attachment to the university because, for a start, it's the only place where my job interview was not an interrogation about whether I was really a historian or a sociologist. The job posting in *The Chronicle of Higher Education*—the clipping of which I still keep in my sock drawer—announced "Political Economy" and invited applications from several possible disciplines. Here, they actually appreciated the denial of disciplinary categories. Thus, I am especially proud of my own department, Social Change and Development. Eight in number, committed to cultivating critical perspectives, and possessed of a rather radical reputation on campus, no finer and more productive group of teachers and scholars exists in the academic world. We have all become something different and more than we started out to be. Hopefully, our students feel the same about their experiences with us.

Of course, the real measure of our success is not whether UWGB and its fellow interdisciplinary institutions have survived *as such*. We were not to be just experiments. We were to be pioneers and revolutionaries. Mistakenly assuming that we have abandoned our original schemes merely because we have matured and toned down our rhetoric, folk at other schools often speak of us in the past tense, in terms like "Remember what they tried to do at UW–Green Bay?"

Admittedly (in certain instances, unfortunately), some things have been lost along the way. For example, while environmental science, design, and policy remain among our strongest offerings, we have given up our original, campuswide, and ahead-of-its-time commitment to the environment—a commitment that had led one national magazine to dub us "Eco U."

Nevertheless, a closer look would reveal not only that many of our initiatives have been flourishing but also that the most intriguing academic endeavors presently underway across academe are, like us, interdisciplinary and problem-focused: cultural and media studies, women and gender studies, historical and area studies, information sciences, environmental sciences, and various professional studies. It is even arguable that the traditional disciplines ceased long ago to be of truly critical value.

I am tempted to close with the words of the English writer John Ruskin that adorn our first academic building: "Therefore when we build . . . let it be such work as our descendants will thank us for: and let us think, as we lay stone on stone, that a time is to come when those stones will be held sacred because our hands have touched them, and that men will say as they look upon the labour and the wrought substance of them, 'See. This our fathers did for us.'"

However, in a spirit even more in keeping with our founders' radical aspirations (and with the arrival this past year of a new chancellor and vice-chancellor), I think we should celebrate not just by commemorating our accomplishments but also by renewing them.

POSTSCRIPT

At the University of Wisconsin–Green Bay we have resolved to find out if a once pioneering and dynamic public university can overcome a decade of institutional drift and lethargy. At the onset of the new century, we have committed ourselves to redeeming our innovative tradition, not by nostalgically trying to restore the past or foolishly jumping onto the distance-education bandwagon but by crafting fresh educational challenges for ourselves. To do so, however, we must not only mobilize ourselves but also persuade the University of Wisconsin Board of Regents to increase our campus budget by more than $4 million.

In "Starting All Over Again," I had expressed more optimism than I probably should have. When I presented the problems our campus faced as challenges, and evidence of the faculty's commitment to face material adversity in an energetic spirit, I may have failed to adequately register just how problematic things had become. The arrival of new administrative leadership had caused me to believe we could, and soon would, resurrect ourselves.

It's unclear how exactly things went wrong: Did we hire the wrong leaders, or did the Board of Regents impose them upon us? In any case, by the late 1980s we found ourselves with a chancellor whose priorities seemed to have little to do with maintaining the university's mission and guaranteeing academic excellence.

I do not exaggerate. Without new resources, the administration raised student numbers beyond a reasonable capacity and imposed a bizarre budget model that rewarded departments by how many students they processed. Nobody had time for imagination and innovation (indeed, we had to abandon certain distinctive features of our curriculum, such as our January term and Senior Seminars program), and it became all the more difficult to pursue scholarship.

After several years, and welcomed retirements, we finally had a chance to recruit a new leadership team in the mid-1990s (as I noted). Fortunately, though our new chancellor, Mark Perkins, made no claim to possess an academic vision for the university, he brought with him a lot of spirit and energy. And with some success he set about addressing campus infrastructural needs and raising monies. But academic life continued to languish and, with excessive workloads and oversized classes, faculty morale declined further. We dropped in the national rankings. I grew impatient. We all knew students deserved better.

Finally, in November 1998, I stood in the Faculty Senate and, following the chancellor's traditional monthly remarks, delivered what the minutes referred to as the "Kaye Challenge." Acknowledging Perkins's achievements, I graciously, but resolutely, urged him to direct his good offices to securing the resources we needed to reverse the university's decline. Depending on the witness, I had either complimented the chancellor or attacked him.

Though it did not seem so at first, Chancellor Perkins "got it." In April 1999 he came before the Faculty Executive Committee and issued a challenge to us. He said that having courted the Board of Regents, he now believed we might be able to secure a dramatic increase in our academic budget starting in the 2001–2003 biennium. Yet he explained that to do so would require strong faculty, staff, and student support *and* an educational vision or idea compelling enough to fire the Regents' imaginations. Moreover, given the system's budget-building schedule, we would have to formulate that idea by summer's end.

There were those who opposed doing anything, either because experience had made them cynical, or because a few months seemed inadequate time to work up a vision capable of garnering campuswide endorsement, or because they just didn't grasp why we needed to fashion new ideas. Nonetheless, a few of us succeeded in pushing for creation of the "Task Force on the Compelling Idea." Led by Vice-Chancellor Howard Cohen, the task force labored hard—fantasizing, arguing, negotiating, compromising, and writing. We issued our report at summer's end, and we felt good about it.

We reaffirmed the university's mission and commitments. We declared that we aspired to prepare students to become "smart, articulate, and engaged citizens and professional practitioners." And we proposed initiatives in *student development* (including first-year seminars, mentoring, and portfolio preparation), *engaged learning* (by way of professional internships and "learning through teaching"), and *citizenship* (through community service, education, and/or research). We both offered original ideas and highlighted various departments' existing practices as endeavors worth pursuing across the campus.

Debate ensued. Resistance came especially from senior faculty in the humanities, environmental sciences, and business. It seemed to have more to do with cynicism and fear than with the worth of the report's particulars.

There were moments when I truly expected the respective governance bodies to reject the entire package. Yet, to my astonishment, the Student Senate not only endorsed it but also agreed to a $300-per-year tuition increase! And the Faculty Senate—having listened patiently to the arguments of the opposition—voted 17–6 in favor. Having pursued the project for so many months, and having seriously prepared myself for defeat, I felt giddy at the outcome.

Of course, the real struggle lies before us. We have no assurances. The chancellor will have to campaign strenuously to secure us the necessary funds. The faculty will have to figure out how to turn grand ideas into real learning experiences—and start doing so before we see any dollars coming our way.

Everyone knows that if the Regents reject our (totally unprecedented) request, the whole effort collapses. Still, most of us believe it's worth taking the risk. If the Regents do come through, we stand a good chance not only to reinvigorate academic life at UW–Green Bay but also to once again serve as pioneers in American higher education.

Chapter 25

BACK IN THE SADDLE, AND LOVING IT: POST-SABBATICAL THOUGHTS

Having been on sabbatical from teaching (1994–95) in favor of research and writing, I thought that after 15 months away I would long to return to the classroom. And yet, as summer vacation wound down, instead of looking forward to the new semester, I found myself fantasizing about another year on my own and imagining all those additional things I could accomplish, if only . . .

Such thinking seriously worried me, for I had decided upon an academic career, most of all, in order to teach. I started to wonder what was occurring to me (besides middle age). However, at the end of my first week back on the job, a couple of delightfully reassuring things happened.

It was after 10:30 P.M. I was waiting for my wife to finish reading the day's *New York Times* so we could retire together. Stretched out on the living room carpet (my preferred television-viewing position), I half-watched "The Tonight Show," hosted by comedian Jay Leno. As usual, Leno was bantering with the show's bandleader, when, all of a sudden, the bandleader stopped him and said, "My pencil broke, what can I do?" On cue, Leno replied with a straight face: "No problem. Bring out the pencil sharpener!" From backstage emerged the mature and beautiful fashion model Lauren Hutton. Renowned for the gap between her two front teeth, Hutton took the pencil, put it in her mouth, and sharpened it to a point; after which she returned it and took a celebrity's bow.

When the laughter and applause died down, Leno turned to the audience and gleefully exclaimed, "What a *great* job I've got." To my happy surprise and relief, I answered him, spontaneously blurting out, "Me, too!"

I went up to bed thinking about what had just transpired. It amused me that I had taken to talking to the television set, but I also found myself thinking back 20 years to how desperately eager I had been to become a

---

Originally appeared in *The Times Higher Education Supplement*, November 17, 1995.

teacher-scholar. Actually, when I first began postgraduate studies, I resisted the idea of teaching. Pursuing a Ph.D. in the mid 1970s (having given up a brief but promising career as an international banker on Wall Street), I wasn't really sure if I could tolerate the pressures and weirdness of academe (or forever "living" among the strange company of academics). But when the opportunity presented itself to serve as a graduate-student instructor, I found the experience exhilarating and I discovered that you really don't know something well until you've tried to teach it to someone else.

Unfortunately, like many of my generation I faced a bleak job market; there just weren't enough positions to go around in 1976 (nor have there been since). But, after a year essentially unemployed, I did secure a 1-year post and then a tenure-track appointment. (Even now—possessed of a titled professorship—one of my worst recurring nightmares involves being unemployed, not only because I have a family to support but also because it would mean being banished from the classroom.)

My late-night thoughts also took me back to my first university job interviews. I had a truly bizarre set of experiences, including encounters with anti-leftism *and* anti-Semitism. I next recalled the question posed to the new assistant professors by the dean of liberal arts at the Minnesota school, St. Cloud State University, where I had latched onto the one-year post. She wanted to know what each of us aspired to accomplish through our teaching. I was somewhat startled by her query and I became all the more anxious when each of my fellow junior colleagues replied rather easily, specifically, and articulately, implying they all had given good thought to the matter.

I, however, was stumped; I hesitated, a bit embarrassed. Finally, I admitted that I really wasn't very sure about what I hoped to achieve because, as I saw it, any information, any facts, I had to pass along could be had from reading books. All I could do, I figured, was to be as engaging and enthusiastic as possible, in hopes that it would be contagious. (It does sometimes seem that students, in their obsession to know "what'll be on the test," have become the character Thomas Gradgrind from Charles Dickens's *Hard Times*: "Now, what I want is, Facts. Teach these boys and girls nothing but Facts. Facts alone are wanted in life." In 1990, while I was visiting English historians Dorothy and Edward Thompson at Rutgers, where they were teaching for a year, Edward humorously remarked to me that his American undergraduate students were making "very unfair demands" on him. "How can I teach them anything, if all they're interested in are 'the facts'?" he said with a grin on his face.)

I went on to explain to the St. Cloud dean and the others that when I thought about who had been my very best teachers, I came up with no single pedagogical type but, instead, a variety of figures. The professors who really excited me about a subject and incited me to learn on my own were, seemingly, eccentrics. By that, I didn't mean they were crazy or simply dramatic actors, eager to entertain the assembled multitude. Rather, I meant they were evidently committed to their subjects, intensely so, and incapable of keeping their thoughts and ideas to themselves. Moreover, they were at the same time intellectually irresistible and so compelling as to lead you to believe that you had an obligation to join them in their endeavors. You left them feeling guilty (and sorry) that you had other things to attend to.

Tired from the week's classroom labors (one forgets how exhausting lecturing can be), and hoping I would soon be asleep, I flipped on a bedside light, fumbled for pen and paper, and jotted down "re Mills" to remind me to look again at C. Wright Mills's *The Sociological Imagination*.[1] Mills had stated it all so smartly: "To some extent, students are a captive audience; and to some extent they are dependent upon their teacher, who is something of a role model to them. His foremost job is to reveal to them how a supposedly self-disciplined mind works. The art of teaching is in considerable part the art of thinking out loud but intelligibly . . . in a classroom the teacher ought to be trying to show how one man thinks—and at the same time reveal what a fine feeling he gets when he does it well."

The following Monday I returned to my three classes, reinvigorated and all the more self-conscious about the task confronting me. In each instance, I began by asking my students what they thought my role was as their professor. Answers varied: "to make learning fun"; "to challenge us"; "to fill us with all the information you can"; "to prepare us to get good jobs." Given the world as it is, I agreed that these were all understandable expectations.

However—to be completely immodest about it—there was one remark that I especially appreciated and that gave me at least a semester's worth of inspiration. One social science student in my favorite course, "Historical Perspectives on Social Change," confessed that her previous experiences in historical studies had "totally" put her off the subject; but she added that I was now making things difficult and she might have to reconsider, for she had never before met anyone "so intense and enthusiastic" about history. I went home that evening, riding high and humming "Back in the Saddle Again."

Chapter 26

SEARCH FOR SIXTIES SOUL

As mailings from the Rutgers University Alumni Association have reminded me, 25 years have passed since my college graduation. Based on my own reaction, I feel confident that upon the arrival of "reunion announcements," my fellow middle-aged alumni could not help but reflect, in both personal and public terms, on the meaning and significance of our student days. More than any other cohort of the decade, we had an awareness of ourselves as part of the "sixties generation."

We were a diverse lot. But, contrary to the claims of the powerful, I think the majority of us shared a deep commitment to American democracy and its possibilities. Raised in the postwar years, we believed that America truly embodied—or, at least, could be made to embody—its proclaimed ideals of liberty, equality, and justice for all. Moreover, we assumed that our nation, conceived in a revolutionary struggle, could not possibly be doing right by fighting an imperial war in Southeast Asia. I continue to believe that, whatever else they might have involved, the movements of the sixties were not campaigns against America, but *for* America.

Of course, as much as we have possessively thought of the sixties as "ours," control of the decade's history was hotly contested even before it came to a close. Powerful interests quickly set about exploiting our experiences by way of clever selection, exaggeration, suppression, and fabrication. As an older colleague warned me: "You can spit at capitalism in protest. But some corporation will harvest it, refine it, and market it. And your mother will buy it for you for Christmas."

I have seen it happen. In 1977, for example, *Playboy* magazine ran the following ad in *The New York Times* in pursuit of advertising revenue: "GOOD NEWS FOR AMERICAN BUSINESS: THOSE YOUNG MEN WHO WOULDN'T SELL OUT IN 1967 ARE BUYING IN IN 1977—You know those young men we're talking about . . . the ones who were marching up and down their campuses protesting a war, forcing a President out

---

Originally appeared in *The Times Higher Education Supplement*, June 14, 1996.

of office, putting barber shops all over America out of business . . . They were remarkable then, intense and totally committed even as teenagers . . . And what's more remarkable about them is that they haven't lost one iota of intensity. They've just redirected it. They've traded the SDS for IBM, GM and ITT . . . Ten years ago they were protesting inequalities they saw in life . . . Today . . . THE PLAYBOY READER. HIS LUST IS FOR LIFE."

Advertising agencies have no monopoly on corrupting history and public memory. Hollywood producers stand equally culpable of using and abusing the sixties (consider the portrayal of the sixties generation in the film *Forrest Gump*). And, as we know all too well, New Right campaigners have spent the last 20 years perversely attributing practically every single national problem to the progressive changes wrought by the several movements of that decade. Such distortions take their toll.

Historians themselves have tried to keep the record straight. A library of work has been accomplished both by activists-turned-professors like Todd Gitlin, *The Sixties: Years of Hope, Days of Rage*; Jim Miller, *Democracy Is in the Streets*; and Maurice Isserman, *If I Had a Hammer*; and by younger folk like Meta Mendel-Reyes, *Reclaiming Democracy*; David Farber, *The Age of Great Dreams*; Kenneth Heineman, *Campus Wars*; and Jim Farrell, *The Spirit of the Sixties*. Moreover, college courses on the sixties have become extremely popular among today's students.[1]

Still, we should not be too sanguine. Can academic scholarship effectively challenge corporate media and the politically powerful? Indeed, as I discovered from the Rutgers Alumni Association's invitations to return for "a fun-filled May reunion weekend," even universities seem capable of suppressing, or at least avoiding, the past.

The first invitation sought to evoke a bit of nostalgia—"It's been years since we walked through Old Queen's Campus and heard the bells of Kirkpatrick Chapel ringing above." It failed to mention that the cluster of buildings constituting Old Queen's housed not classrooms or student residences but the university administration, and, aside from the chapel, only on rare occasions did we ever step inside one of them. It also failed to note the most important of those rare occasions—the student occupation of Old Queen's in May 1970, following the killings at Kent State.

Along with the invitation came a questionnaire asking our preferred "Reunion Parade uniform: T-shirt, sweater, blazer, baseball cap, shorts, and/or sweatshirt"? This made me snicker and wonder about the reunion committee. A "Reunion Parade uniform"? However much it may have seemed that my generation dressed in a uniform fashion—work boots, jeans, and flannel shirts in winter; sandals, jeans, and T-shirts in summer—most of us did our damnedest to stay out of a uniform.

I imagined the committee consisted of former ROTC cadets; and, on second thought, I hoped it was, for it would have meant they had survived the war years. Yet, on further thought, I figured that anybody who had worn a uniform would never want to again. That led me to the conclusion that the committee was composed of those Young Republican types who had avidly supported the war but had done everything they could to avoid having themselves drafted into it.

A later mailing, directed to all the classes of Rutgers graduates, provided a list of reunion activities, including: tennis and golf outings, campus tours, gift and estate planning seminars, luncheons and dinners, musical performances, and an evening at the Stress Factory Comedy Club. I was now convinced that Republicans were running the show.

More intriguing for what they ignored than for what they included, the reunion announcements could have been addressed to any class of graduates a generation later. Who knows what went on in the minds of the committee members? Maybe they just didn't want to offend anybody. Or maybe they felt embarrassed by acts committed a quarter-century ago and were now trying to repress or cover up memories of radical politics and/or sex, drugs, and rock 'n roll. Or perhaps, like the corporate execs and New Right politicos (which some of them no doubt are), they remained anxious about what a more critical remembrance of the sixties might entail, that is, what it might demand in the face of the politics of the day.

Are the sixties finished, kept alive merely in the memories of a graying generation of radicals? Yes. But the struggles are not. And, just as the aspirations of the sixties were linked to earlier generations' efforts, I am confident that another generation will arise to renew our campaigns to realize America's finest possibilities.

In fact, about the time I received yet another mailing from the reunion committee, I also received one from the AFL-CIO announcing "Union Summer." In the spirit of Freedom Summer, which sent 1000 college students south to register black voters in 1964, 1500 students will spend their 1996 vacations in cities around the nation working with labor unions for workplace rights and social justice. The sixties may be finished, but the nineties are not over yet.

Chapter 27

A YANK IN LONDON— OR LOVE AND CLASS STRUGGLES

It was 25 years ago, in September 1971, that I first landed in Britain to study for a master's degree. In honor of the 25th anniversary of the London *Times Higher Education Supplement* (THES), I offer these personal reminiscences . . .

My narrative begins in 1970, when, as a "junior-year-abroad" student at the National University of Mexico, I came across a poster announcing "Scholarships to London." An American, I knew I had no hope of securing British Council support (or, given my grades, a Rhodes Scholarship), but the idea of studying in London quickly captured my imagination. And, when I discovered that foreign student fees were a mere £250/$500, even the cost of living in London seemed manageable. (Still, in order to make it a reality, I had to work full time as a publishing assistant at the social science magazine *Transaction* for much of my senior year at Rutgers. Fortunately, as a History Department honors research student, I could arrange my schedule to accommodate the work hours. Anyhow, I saved a lot and borrowed the rest.)

My British "education" started en route. Taking my seat on the "student charter," I heard a woman calling out the seat number next to mine. Speaking *English*, not American, she was, to my great surprise, black. Having foolishly assumed that all Britons were white, that the only blacks I would meet would be West Indian or African immigrants, I realized I had a lot to learn.

First, I had to find somewhere to live. I stayed a week at London House (a private trust's hostel for British Commonwealth and American students). I found the resident Australians most welcoming and congenial, which eventually led to my second "ethnic" surprise.

Hunting for a "flat," I continually received advice from the English to "Stay away from Earl's Court . . . it's a really rough area." As a New Yorker,

---

Originally appeared in *The Times Higher Education Supplement*, September 6, 1996.

I immediately figured such warnings had something to do with race. Just imagine my face when, having mentioned this to my Aussie mates, they informed me, laughing hysterically, that "the Poms" (as they called the English) were actually counseling me to stay away from the likes of them! The English apparently saw folks from "down under" as a bunch of drunken louts.

I ended up living on the north side of Hyde Park, in Bayswater, a multicultural neighborhood populated by Greeks, Indians, and various other Eurasian folk. Although I'd never eaten Indian food before, it soon became one of my favorite cuisines. Also new for me—all the more so because Rutgers had been an all-male college—my roommate, a Canadian art student, was a woman. Heather and I became good friends, somewhat like brother and sister—which her parents didn't quite believe until they stayed with us for a week. Our landlord, a Polish count who had a most beautiful wife, had served during the Second World War as a pilot in the exiled Polish Air Force. The elderly English housekeeper was definitely batty. Sounds like the ingredients for a television comedy, no?

Pursuing an M.A. in Area Studies, I had courses at University College London (UCL), the Institute of Latin American Studies, and the London School of Economics (LSE). I soon developed my own daily rituals. Going by "tube"—that is, the underground (subway)—to UCL, I would always complete my commute by entering through the main hall and bidding "good morning" to the auto-iconic, utilitarian philosopher Jeremy Bentham. Heading by double-decker bus to the LSE in the Aldwych, I would regularly stop in Piccadilly Circus to play the slot machines, the penny one-armed bandits. If I won, I would then hop on another bus for the remainder of the trip; if not, I would quickly walk the relatively short distance. Either way, I never failed to arrive on time for my LSE seminar (in a building just opposite "Ye Olde Curiosity Shoppe").

I found my fellow students a most impressive lot. Because of my undergraduate studies, and having lived twice in Latin America, I naturally assumed I was better prepared. Again, I was the fool. I may have "known" more, but my British colleagues definitely thought more critically and argued more effectively. While I wrote reports, they wrote essays. Fortunately, one of the younger lecturers, a Marxist, was a very smart and kindly guy and, through a series of clever research assignments, he aimed me in a more critical direction. The questions he posed also instigated my thinking along Marxian lines.

It took me a while to get used to British academic manners. They were very different from American academic manners, and very different from what I had expected. Arguments seemed much more pointed *and* more personal. And yet, when we would break for coffee at 11 or tea at 4, the discussions and the participants mellowed. We would still talk, and the conversations remained animated, but we would stop arguing. Civility, I think they call it. Evening lectures and gatherings at the Institute afforded further engagements, but peanuts and sherry made them especially warm and friendly occasions.

You can take the Yank out of the States, but you can't keep him from behaving like an American. In my young, forward, and overly democratic manner, I treated the Institute's quarters as if I owned them. This rather annoyed the faculty and staff. I would poke about and ask questions I probably shouldn't have. Of course, it served *me* well. Not long after meeting Lorna Stewart, the Institute's new executive officer, I bluntly asked her if she had a boyfriend. She said she did—yet I persisted and she soon broke up with him. We've been married for 23 years now.

Britain changed my life in a variety of ways. Like so many of my generation, I had firmly radical-democratic politics. But in London, with its (then) vibrant left culture, I began to develop socialist sensibilities (and the government's planned blackouts during the 1972 miners' strike encouraged Lorna's and my romance and led me to better appreciate the intimate connection between love and the class struggle).

Depending on the day, I would either lunch with student colleagues at the LSE or with Lorna at a local pub, where I'd have "bangers, beans, and mash" (sausage, beans, and mashed potatoes) with a cider to drink, or at UCL, where I just loved the chips (french fries). Afterward, I would spend an inordinate amount of time in The Economist Bookshop at LSE or Dillon's Bookshop at UCL. I would browse the shelves as if they were the "new arrivals" section of the library. I also bought too many books (particularly Penguin paperbacks, which at least were rightly priced for a student budget).

I wrote my dissertation during July and August. Summer seemed even hotter than in New York. But it turned out the reason I felt so warm was that I had come down with what the English call "glandular fever," that is, mononucleosis (aka the "kissing disease"). Rather than stay at home in bed, I napped a lot in the Institute's comfortable seminar room and somehow finished the project on time.

I regularly attended the theater and, with Lorna's encouragement, the Royal Ballet on occasion. And, though my funds were limited, I did get to travel a bit. In addition to visiting Oxford and Cambridge, I went out to Salisbury and Stonehenge, down to Brighton to see the sea, up to Birmingham and the Midlands, and over to Aberystwyth on the Welsh coast. Student airfares enabled me to visit Geneva, Paris, and Amsterdam. But I loved London the most and fully subscribed to the proposition that "when you're tired of London, you're tired of life." I remember saying that whereas Paris may be a city for artists and intellectuals, London is definitely a city for students and scholars.

From the collections and talks at the British Museum (I saw the once-in-a-lifetime King Tut exhibit), Royal Institute of International Affairs, and International Institute of Strategic Studies, to the showings at the ICA (Institute of Contemporary Art) and more informal venues, London seemed one big campus. On Sundays, Lorna and I would cover the city on foot. I desperately wanted to stay on for a Ph.D., and London did accept me. But, already burdened with student loans, I was flat broke and couldn't afford another year. I vividly recall searching the pages of the then-new THES, hoping to find a fellowship.

Upon returning to the States, I confess to having taken a position on Wall Street with Lloyds Bank as their very first *American* international-lending-officer trainee. By all accounts, my future looked bright. To everyone but me, that is. I had political doubts about it; I found the daily grind inhibited intellectual activity; and I hated "suiting" up. When the opportunity arose of a doctoral fellowship at Louisiana State University, I grabbed it. I love saying I went from LSE to LSU.

We get back to Britain every couple of years. In fact, around 1980 I shifted from Latin American to British studies. And, of course, much else has changed in the past quarter-century. Nevertheless, I continually recommend to my most capable students that they think about graduate study in Britain and, though overseas student fees have skyrocketed, I have persuaded several to do it. So far, like their mentor, not one has regretted it.

Chapter 28

HISTORY AND THE GREAT BALLOON DEBATE

Do you remember the Great Balloon Debate staged in the pages of *The Times Higher Education Supplement* (THES) in February 1996? I found it so fascinating I have taken to producing versions of it with my first-year students. Those occasions have been not only entertaining, they have been, as well, real learning experiences—for me at least as much as for my students. They have revealed far more than the relative popularity of selected scholarly disciplines. The ensuing discussions have taught me a lot about my students and their generation's worldview. What I have learned has encouraged me, frightened me, *and* reminded me once again of the challenges my colleagues and I confront.

I should start by refreshing your memories of the original Great Balloon Debate. Behaving like the gods on Mount Olympus, the THES's editors posed the following question: "Seven scientists/Six social scientists/Seven humanists are plunging to earth in an overloaded hot air balloon. All but one of them must jump off if the balloon is to be light enough for just one to float to safety. But who should be the lucky survivor?"

In successive weeks the editorial deities pitted the respective science (particle physics, physics, ecobiology, engineering, chemistry, molecular biology, mathematics), social science (sociology, economics, political science, psychology, anthropology, geography), and humanities (classics, religion, fine art, modern languages, philosophy, history, English) disciplines against each other in a grand game of survival. First, the disciplines from each area faced off in a winner-takes-all battle; then, the three winners competed to see which of them would prevail in the final perilous confrontation. Champions were selected to represent their disciplines, and we readers were asked to choose the survivor by voting on-line. Though only a game, intellectual honor was at stake. And, given the meager material rewards of academe, honor is everything, no?

Originally appeared in *The Times Higher Education Supplement*, December 19, 1997.

My own university is an interdisciplinary institution. So, I immediately thought that all the disciplines should perish. And yet I could not resist following the debate. In fact, I not only joined in by voting for my favorites, I also proceeded to put together a Social Science Great Balloon Debate on my own campus that very semester.

I invited faculty trained in anthropology, economics, geography, political science, psychology, and sociology to appear before my 150-student lecture course and present 5-minute statements explaining why their particular discipline should survive while the others sacrificed themselves. My colleagues' commitments and murderous instincts quickly revealed themselves. Each not only spoke eloquently for his or her discipline, each also seemed willing, if not eager, to throw the others out of the balloon.

Our results differed from those in the THES. Whereas, in the newspaper, geography triumphed among the social sciences, at UW–Green Bay, anthropology prevailed. Corresponding with the THES editors, I learned that in each area the practitioners of at least one of the disciplines apparently had organized and mobilized to successfully save themselves: in science, particle physicists had done so; in the humanities, religion folk; and in the social sciences, geographers.

Here in the American Midwest, what truly determined the outcome was the strength of the case made by our competing anthropologist, Lynn Walter. Though I would not have saved anthropology, my students did, persuaded by Professor Walter's argument that the skills and sensibilities that her discipline cultivates become all the more invaluable in a complex, diverse, and multicultural world. Indeed, my students' deliberations impressed and pleased me. Critically developed, their thinking and sentiments seemed to bode well for the future.

We had so much fun, I decided to restage the debate this year. However, I set it up differently. Instead of recruiting colleagues, I arranged for my students to debate the matter among themselves. I set out the problem and gave my students a week to decide individually which discipline should survive and to prepare their respective arguments. To launch the balloon I provided definitions of each discipline, but I told the students they could use outside resources to help them make their choices and cases. Plus, I added my own favorite, history, to the passenger list.

I was in for a shock. When my students reported back, the overwhelming majority had chosen to save history. I got terribly excited and allowed myself to believe that I was witnessing the end of American students' lack of interest in the subject. But my students soon disabused me of the fantasy. Their selection of history reflected not a return to the discipline but, simply, youthful resourcefulness and good old American pragmatism.

Aside from the few who really were "turned on" to historical studies, most—as they over and over again explained—had chosen to rescue the discipline because it apparently encompasses just about "everything" (at least as it is presently practiced). They figured that if we saved history, we could eventually rediscover all the other disciplines. I now felt very ambivalent. Though it disappointed me that my students were not clamoring for historical education, I could not fail to appreciate their cleverness. Still, there's more to it.

It disturbed me even more that political science had only a couple of advocates (and they revealingly expressed Machiavellian ambitions). True, I would probably join the majority in dumping it—but only after we had joyfully hurled economics and psychology overboard. Nevertheless, it turned out that my students were willing to give up far more than the academic discipline. They actually spoke as if they were prepared to junk politics and political questions altogether. As more than one of them put it: "Who cares about politics?!"—confident that the answer was "nobody."

The more we talked, the clearer it became that although my students value history as a record of human experience—like a gigantic World Wide Web of the past to be called on-line when you need it—it is not something to which they feel any intimate connection. To them, "politics" appeared to be an essentially irrelevant, if not worthless, enterprise.

When I asked them which discipline they would prefer to study, the greatest number replied "psychology," as you might expect in this therapeutic age of ours. They declared a fascination with the workings of the human mind and a belief that understanding it better would lead to individual *and* social progress.

My students did voice concerns about social issues and problems. Yet they hesitated to discuss them in terms of acknowledged inequalities of power and wealth, and they all but refused to consider addressing them by altering collective social arrangements, apparently believing it would be futile to even try to do so. In short, the powers that be will be pleased to learn that although my students feel unsettled about the way things are, and believe improvement remains possible, they apparently defer to the notion that we have arrived at the "end of history," the conservative claim that we can develop freedom, equality, and democracy no more than we have already.

Personal political preferences aside, I have always believed that although history and social science cannot tell us what to do, their study should enable us to understand the world, to appreciate that the way things are is not necessarily the way they have to be, and to critically consider alternatives. The most recent rendition of the Great Balloon Debate indicates my colleagues and I clearly have our work cut out for us.

Chapter 29

THE NEST STARTS TO EMPTY—
OR YOU CAN SEE HER FROM MONTICELLO

I entered the academic year 1998–99 in a new role—not as a student, not merely as a professor, but as the *parent* of a university student. My wife Lorna and I took our first child, Rhiannon, to the University of Virginia to commence her freshman year in the School of Architecture (A-School). The nest has started to empty.

The process began a year ago, when Rhiannon applied to Virginia "early decision" (whereby a student applies early and *only* to his or her first-choice university, rather than later to several, in hopes of securing an offer in December instead of months later, in April). Smartly, the University of Virginia—UVA, or "the university" as Virginians call it—accepted her, so we had more than enough time to prepare ourselves materially *and* emotionally. Or so I thought.

The prospect of Rhiannon studying at Virginia thrilled me. Envisioned, designed, and built by Thomas Jefferson in Charlottesville, within view of Monticello, Jefferson's beloved mountaintop estate, the university lies not far from the Shenandoah Mountains and possesses a gorgeous campus, referred to as "the grounds."

Moreover, Virginia ranks "first" among American public universities; its School of Architecture stands among the top ten in the country; and, in the revolutionary spirit of the university's founder, the A-School has taken the lead in the Sustainable Design movement, under the leadership of the widely heralded "green dean," William McDonough.[1]

Securing early acceptance, Rhiannon avoided the long anxious period of waiting to hear from admissions offices; but I now realize it also meant a longer period of my trying to deny the fact that our baby would be leaving home.

We spent the spring and summer in a seemingly relaxed manner. Lorna and I reminisced with Rhiannon about our own first-year experiences,

---

Originally appeared in *The Times Higher Education Supplement*, October 2, 1998.

Lorna's at Birmingham (England), mine at Rutgers. After numerous deliberations, we resolved to make the 1000-mile journey to Virginia with Rhiannon's clothes, tchotchkes, books, and CDs by flying to my sister's home near Washington, D.C., and renting a car for the 2-hour drive to Charlottesville.

While Rhiannon's younger sister, Fiona, started asserting sole claim to their shared bedroom, I evaded thinking about her big sister's departure by approaching it in a scholarly fashion. I studied the UVA catalog. I picked up Guy Wilson's illustrated monograph, *Thomas Jefferson's Academical Village*; a couple of Jefferson biographies; and a collection of Jefferson's writings. As well, I bought Roger Lewis's *Architect?—A Candid Guide to the Profession* and innumerable design magazines to acquaint myself with the latest developments.[2]

I threw myself into the whole thing even more than Rhiannon did. She just wanted to enjoy her last several months of high school. However, in late July, Lorna and Rhiannon finally confronted the tasks of organizing accounts and selecting what was to stay and what was to go. I urged traveling light, for my impending assignment was to lug all the stuff up the residence-hall stairs in the Southern heat and humidity (fortunately, Rhiannon chose to get a laptop computer rather than a desktop). Also, along with piles of material arriving from UVA and assorted vendors, Rhiannon eventually received a letter from her roommate-to-be, a Hong Kong Chinese student who had orders to pursue something "practical" but personal aspirations to read linguistics.

The night before we set out, I took the family to Rhiannon's favorite steakhouse, after which we spent the evening playing our favorite board games (just thinking about it brings tears to my eyes). I intended to give Rhiannon lots of sage advice, but never got around to it. Anyhow, she'd heard it all before.

Arriving in sunny Charlottesville, we joined the masses of nervous-yet-hopeful parents and 18-year-olds. Students eyed each other warily and then introduced themselves; parents, passing each other on the flights of stairs, burdened down with cases and boxes, shared their own anxieties by joking about serving as their kids' "bearers" and about how much stuff had to be squeezed into such tiny rooms. I remarked how "education is wasted on the young," and wondered to myself if all my perspiration would reduce the moisture flowing to my tear ducts later in the day.

Sweating from our labors, we attended a welcome address by the university's president, John Casteen. Instinctively hostile towards administrators, I nevertheless liked him and what he had to say (was I just being naïve and getting taken in?).

One could feel Jefferson's presence everywhere. At the A-School, Dean McDonough impressed me by speaking of contemporary architecture's revolutionary challenges, especially the humanistic and environmental ones. Suppressing the pain of separation, I kept repeating how exciting Rhiannon's next 4 years would be, unaware she had just told her mom that she felt rather intimidated by the scale and grandeur of the place.

Back at the residence hall, Lorna and Rhiannon clearly did not want to part; but convinced that I would be the most upset, I hurried our farewells. Fortunately, our friends Eileen Boris and Nelson Lichtenstein, who teach in the UVA History Department, had invited us for dinner, so I had an excuse to move things along.

Kindly, Eileen and Nelson had chilled a couple of beers to refresh and console us, and they promised to check regularly on Rhiannon's progress. I spent the evening arguing politics with their brilliant, but anti-academic, high school–aged son, Dan, which distracted me from thinking about my own child for a little while. Driving up to D.C. later that evening, I asked Lorna if we should ring Rhiannon (hoping Lorna would say yes), but she thought we should resist doing so.

Starting the new term back in Wisconsin, I looked at my first-year students and saw dozens of daughters and sons, and I wondered how their parents were faring. We commiserated with our close friends, the Kuritzes, who themselves had just returned from taking their firstborn son to the University of Colorado to start engineering school. And my secretary—who had previously worked in our university's counseling center—sympathetically referred me to *Letting Go: A Parents' Guide to Today's College Experience*.[3] Meanwhile, Rhiannon keeps us informed by phone and e-mail (God bless the Internet!), and we look forward to Virginia's autumn Family Weekend.

Chapter 30

COLLEGIAL PLEASURES

These days, American academics rarely speak publicly about the delights of what the English call "donnish life." No doubt we fear it would afford ammunition to our enemies, those bureaucrats and executives who insist that professors "have it cushy" and those conservatives who accuse us of corruption. We gripe, complain, and protest. We feel besieged, and we truly have every reason to do so. The culture wars may be waning, but the codification, commodification, and proletarianization of higher education intensify.

But does our silence on the joys of academe do us any good? Apparently concerned that we've allowed ourselves to sound like, if not become, a bunch of sourpusses, James Axtell, professor of ethnohistory at the College of William and Mary, has broken the taboo and authored *The Pleasures of Academe*.[1]

Axtell frames his book as a response to our antagonists. But he writes more affirmatively than defensively. Without conceding anything to our critics, he reminds us of the simple, yet rich, enjoyments of our vocation. In chapters combining professional reflection and personal recollection, he treats not only serious questions like the demands and intrigues of scholarship and "what makes a university great?" but also far more entertaining subjects like bibliolatry, interdisciplinarity, college sports, college towns, and academic family vacations. I read snippets to my family, rightly figuring they would empathize with Axtell's wife and children.

Unfortunately, Axtell does not really get into the pleasures of academic comradeship. Admittedly, in the course of endless meetings, and the even more dreadful peer reviews, friendships can be severely tested. But, in a country the size of America, pursuing a career that inevitably takes you far from your parental home, departmental colleagues and their families can become like kinfolk, especially at holiday times.

Originally appeared in *The Times Higher Education Supplement*, February 2, 1999.

Every year, our family celebrates Labor Day, Thanksgiving Day, Memorial Day and July 4th with a couple of my colleagues, anthropologist Tony Galt and historian Craig Lockard, and their wives and children. After 20 years of doing so, we're all essentially an extended family (though I think we get along far better than the usual assortment of such). I particularly relish those moments when the older kids, having put up with us for so long, come home from college ready and eager to educate their professorial parents and elders. As the youngest of the three profs, I dread the possibility that our friends will take early retirement and seek out warmer climes than Wisconsin.

Academic comradeship can even transcend seemingly immense obstacles like disciplinary boundaries, age differences, and political antagonisms. Here I not only join with Axtell in breaking the aforementioned taboo but I also reveal my participation in a most secret society, which, since 1987, has convened three times annually to address the issues of the university, higher education, America, and the globe. The group is so audacious we usually tackle the past as much as the present!

Our mysterious, all-male society's membership is so unfathomable, I doubt my revelation will be taken seriously by those who recognize its membership. Our clandestine club consists of scientist Dave Jowett, humanist Jerry Rodesch, and social scientist me. Respectively, we are a conservative Liverpudlian in his 60s, a liberal Wisconsinite in his 50s, and a socialist New Yorker in his 40s.

Consider what I suffer in hopes of solving the world's problems. On one side, I confront an excitable working-class "Scouser" (yet another affectionate term to refer to someone from Liverpool). He preferred history but felt compelled to study biology and then, after a stint with the Colonial Office in Uganda, came to the United States on a postdoctoral fellowship, became a conservative in the 1960s, and served a term as our university's vice-chancellor in the 1980s. And, on the other, I face a relaxed midwestern "cheesehead" from a labor-union family who, having served a stint with the U.S. State Department in Florence, returned home to pursue a professorial career in the humanities and exults in belittling the excesses of social science. (I do love those guys.)

To avoid detection, surveillance, and distraction, we hold our never-quite-long-enough, five-hour sessions at a Mexican bar and restaurant located some miles from campus. And we always depart after dark. Furthermore, we only pause in our deliberations when ordering our fajitas or another round of Bass Ale. Call us callous, in view of the urgency and weight of the issues we confront. But we definitely have one "helluva good time."

By 10 P.M., we've just warmed up. Had we another few hours in session, I think we would either figure out how to actually solve the world's crises, or end up never speaking to each other again. Fortunately, spouses and families beckon.

It's amazing. Nothing ever gets resolved, and yet I always leave feeling really good. (Lest you jump to conclusions, please note that we stop drinking well before we head our separate ways.) I wouldn't want my co-conspirators to get inflated egos, but I always leave thinking that as wrong or inadequate as their views are politically, they do know far more than I do. Of course, my dad always said that the smartest thing you can do is to make sure you have friends who are smarter than you are.

OK, I've come clean. I love the academic life—not just for the excitements of teaching, writing, and service but also for the many other special pleasures it affords. Indeed, when you think about it, the worst problems lie not in academe but in those institutions of the corporate world that, while they pay so well, fail to engender real pleasure and comradeship.

Chapter 31

FELICITY AT THE BARRICADES

One of television's most popular new series, "Felicity," presents the trials and tribulations of a bright and attractive California 18-year-old who has gone east to study at the fictitious "University of New York." (Note that NYU would not sell or lend its name to the producers, perhaps fearing a bad image if the show got too kinky.) Arguably, the show's appearance last September reflects more than corporate ambitions to capture teen viewers. With the culture wars abating, the media once again have focused their higher-education attentions on youthful students rather than aging professors.

Most of the time, coverage has been predictable and the news discouraging. However, as the academic year unfolded, a more complex picture of undergraduate attitudes, aspirations, and prospects began to materialize. While we should avoid foolish optimism, if we think about the parentage of today's students, the possibilities become even more intriguing and the future wonderfully less predictable than our governing elites have led us to believe.

At the outset, we read almost everywhere how a "culture of disengagement" characterizes contemporary student life. Confirming our own unscientific observations and anxieties, research revealed that undergraduates spend fewer hours studying and more time off-campus, socializing, or working in paid employment (either to cover tuition and living expenses or to enhance their lifestyles). Portending worse to come, incoming freshmen state that they found high school utterly boring, possess little interest in learning, have no inclination to social activism, and view their studies as simply a means of securing higher incomes.

Undergraduates supposedly have disengaged not only from their studies but also from their traditional extracurricular activities. Arthur Levine and Jeannette Cureton lament in the June 1998 issue of *Change Magazine*, in an article entitled "Collegiate Life: An Obituary": "Higher education is

---

Originally appeared in *The Times Higher Education Supplement*, July 2, 1999.

not as central to the lives of today's undergraduates as it was to previous generations. Increasingly, college is just one of a multiplicity of activities in which they are engaged every day."

In the wake of such tales, student "partying" habits surfaced as the hot topic, briefly leading one to think that perhaps students hadn't changed all that much. However, one survey gave real cause for worry. On-campus drug and alcohol arrests recently have increased significantly across the country and, though officials claimed it mostly had to do with their new determination to "crack down" on offenders, campus health-service folk related that more and more students confess they drink "to get drunk."

The New York Times reported that in reaction to just such developments, student groups on a variety of campuses have called upon administrators to reassert *in loco parentis*, wherein "educators serve as stand-in parents." And *The Chronicle of Higher Education* has noted a significant increase in applications for admission to Christian fundamentalist colleges. Applicants interviewed said they wanted clear rules and controls, not simply because they didn't trust themselves, but all the more so because they didn't want to contend with more libertine types.

Whether represented as hedonists or puritans, students seemed an uninspired lot. However, spring brought forth other, fresher images as well. From out of the ranks of those very same disengaged materialists, committed idealists emerged to start shaking things up.

Students at more than 20 universities around the nation—including Duke, Georgetown, Holy Cross, Yale, Michigan, Wisconsin, and Berkeley—staged rallies, teach-ins, and sit-ins protesting sweatshops and other labor issues. As *The New York Times* story declared: "Activism Surges at Campuses Nationwide, and Labor Is at Issue" (March 29).

Such actions recalled the 1960s, but with certain glaring differences. In the sixties, student protestors regularly found themselves at odds with labor. Today, student demonstrators align themselves *with* labor. In particular, students have demanded an end to the arrangement whereby universities license the right to manufacture sweatshirts, T-shirts, and caps bearing their logos to companies dealing with overseas sweatshops.

At some schools, like Harvard and the University of Virginia, students also have demonstrated in support of "living wage" campaigns pursued by the lowliest-paid university employees, janitors and cafeteria workers. And on many campuses students have rallied in support of diversity, affirmative action, and gay rights.

Student activism seems to have arisen out of nowhere. But we should appreciate its possible origins. In 1996, the AFL-CIO's new leadership instituted "Union Summer," a program in which 1500 students each summer have served as interns in union- and community-organizing drives.

Some students have gone on to become professional organizers; almost all have returned to campus eager to mobilize fellow students in support of labor.

There's more to it, however. These are "our kids," that is, the children of the sixties generation. Predictably, our own contradictions express themselves in their lives. We may pride ourselves on our political radicalism. But let's not forget that our generation also provided cohorts for the conservative Young Americans for Freedom and the ensuing New Right movement. We may nostalgically revel in our cultural rebelliousness, but we "boomers" have turned into a most materialist lot.

And yet, in spite of our hypocrisies and failings, we may well have imbued at least some of our offspring with utopian impulses. They question, volunteer, challenge, and may yet seek to change the present order of things for the better. We should not underestimate them.

Indeed, whether or not this new student movement truly takes root, spreads, and becomes a major force for change, the new student activists already have accomplished something of potentially radical import. They have helped to re-create a progressive alliance between intellectuals and labor.

I wonder if the upcoming television season will see sophomore Felicity joining a picket line, sitting-in at the dean's office, and signing up for Union Summer 2000.

Chapter 32

PILGRIMS WITH TALES TO TELL

The Second International Congress of "History Under Debate" met July 14–18, 1999, in Santiago de Compostela, Spain. More than 500 scholars from around the world gathered to assess twentieth-century historiography and to deliberate where we should take the discipline. I came away having enjoyed myself immensely and, based on the exchanges I participated in, feeling rather hopeful about history's prospects.

My wife, Lorna, younger daughter, Fiona, and I arrived in Santiago several days early to explore Galicia and practice our Spanish. Festivity abounded. Xacobeo, the annual pilgrimage to Santiago—the city of Saint James, Spain's patron saint—was already underway. In fact, the congress organizers put us up in a seventeenth-century monastery in the medieval heart of the city, right next to the cathedral and main square, remarkably named, long ago, the Plaza of the Workers.

Adding to the excitement, Santiago is this year's official "European City of Culture." Every evening at 11 P.M., the city's plazas were transformed into venues for jazz, classical, or folk concerts. Lorna and Fiona especially enjoyed the flirtatious "Tuna de Derecho" (the law students' traditional musical group), which performed nightly to enthusiastic crowds under the arches in the main square. I can personally attest that Galicia deserves its fame for seafood—octopus, squid, scallops, mussels, shrimp . . . And, for dessert or a snack, I highly recommend the splendid *tarta de Santiago* (almond cake).

My enthusiasm for the local scene and delicacies clearly pleased my hosts; but they had brought me to Spain to talk about history, not music and menus. So, when the congress opened—while Lorna and Fiona continued to tour, shop, and flirt—I got serious. Which is not to say I stopped enjoying myself.

I hate to sound provincial, but I had never participated in a conference as grand as this gathering. Led by University of Santiago medievalist Carlos

---

Originally appeared in *The Times Higher Education Supplement*, August 27, 1999.

Barros, the organizers had evidently worked hard to bring it together. Professor Barros had secured sizable financial support from the regional government of Galicia. That was no mean feat. The provincial president is none other than Manuel Fraga Iribarne, leader of Spain's conservatives and a former protégé of the late dictator Francisco Franco. Surreally, Fraga himself gave the welcoming address (presumably prepared by others), quoting none other than the world's premier Marxist historian, Eric Hobsbawm.

Each day opened with a plenary address. Thus, after many years of admiring their work, I was able to meet and hear the renowned Mexican historian Enrique Florescano speak on his own country's history and memory (actually diverse memories) and the senior American historiographer George Iggers on postmodernist history and its problems. Following each morning's plenary, there were three concurrent 4-hour sessions, consisting of eight 15-minute presentations plus debate. At midafternoon we broke for a two-hour *comida* (big meal), later returning to work for yet another set of 4-hour sessions.

Such lengthy sessions were demanding (especially to the jet-lagged). At the close of the first day, I commiserated with a fellow American about how the length of the sessions seemed almost punishing, however fascinating the several presentations. And I jokingly asked when Catholic Spain had succumbed to the Protestant ethic. Indeed, the only redeeming feature of the fact that I could not—for medical reasons—partake of the local white wine served at lunch was that it enabled me to stay alert through those evening sessions. I would have relished a *siesta*.

Since I hadn't spoken Spanish intensively in almost 25 years, it surprised me how quickly the language returned. My Latin colleagues generously complimented my competence (acquired years ago in Ecuador and Mexico), but I could tell that Lorna—who received her degree in Spanish at the University of Birmingham and had spent a year in Madrid before we met—impressed them all the more with her Castilian fluency. Fortunately, Fiona, though hesitant to speak in Spanish (having, so far, completed only 2 years of high school study), has already developed a solid vocabulary. I often turned to her when my mind drew a blank on a particular word.

Though the sessions were demanding, the papers—and responses from the audience—were well worth hearing, especially those delivered at the roundtables. Having focused on American studies for the past several years, I was keen to learn of scholarly and pedagogical developments from Paris to Patagonia. I tried my best not to be too impressed by French historian Jacques Revel, current director of the *Annales*, the world's foremost school of history, but I failed. Understanding not a word of French, I still found it helpful to occasionally turn off the headset affording simultaneous translation in order to better "feel" Revel's words and better sense the spirit in which he offered them. I do wish I knew the language. French sounds so intellectual. But Revel and I were later able to converse, for he speaks impeccable English and has traveled widely.

I really liked the Spanish historians and their graduate students (several of the former had served in the opposition to Franco as youngsters). In spite of the bleak university job prospects (apparently worse even than in the United States), the graduate students so loved history and ideas they could not resist pursuing doctoral studies. They were most welcoming of this American, and very eager to share their thoughts.

It was also a pleasure to finally meet Cuban historians, some of whom, to my surprise, had visited the States. I had looked forward to hearing about Chinese historiography 10 years after the grand demonstrations and ensuing brutalities and tragedies in Tiananmen Square, but, sadly, the talk by the Beijing historian sounded more like party propaganda than scholarship.

The Argentinian historians of my own generation moved me in particular. They had survived the dictatorship years, some of them in exile or jail. They had lost colleagues and comrades. And yet they remained determined intellectuals, eager to connect their work to projects for justice and change. I was honored to appear with them on panels treating "Historians and Power" and "Historians and Commitment." For all my professed radicalism, I felt like a naive innocent alongside them. Nevertheless, they seemed to appreciate my words, particularly my plenary address, "Fanning the Spark of Hope in the Past" [Chapter 21]. Meeting them inspired my delivery.

It struck me that the historians present shared certain concerns, regardless of their national origins and political sympathies. They spoke anxiously about fragmentation, both of the discipline and of the grand narratives of past and present. They wondered about the duties of historians, morally and politically. And they were eager to hear about ways that historians might speak more effectively to extra-academic publics.

Congress director Carlos Barros himself urged participants to see themselves as part of a movement. He called upon us to think globally, conceive of the present moment in terms of "civilizational" change, and consider what kind of constructive role historians might play in the making of the new global society. I dissented somewhat on his portrait, or interpretation, of contemporary history, seeing in his remarks a too ready disavowal of Marxian and critical understandings and an eagerness to defer to the classical *Annales* emphasis on the idea of "civilization" (which stresses transnational cultural and economic life at the expense of the study of politics and power). He chided me in a collegial way for occasionally sounding like an American patriot (which I don't deny).

I particularly argued for a critical, committed, democratic historiography. No consensus emerged. But that was fine. We had made pilgrimage to Santiago to debate history, not wrap it up. It thrilled me simply to know that we were openly debating matters of theory and politics in a country where merely a generation ago it would have been out of the question.

Chapter 33

TURNING 50 ON THE EVE OF 2000

I remember lying awake at night as a child trying to fathom growing up and older. I specifically recall thinking about the year 2000, and calculating that on the eve of the new millennium I would turn 50. My sleeplessness had nothing to do with futuristic visions, science-fiction fantasies, or alien-invasion nightmares (actually, my standard 1950s nightmare had Godzilla dropping atomic bombs on my elementary school). No, my sleeplessness had to do simply with thoughts of my own mortality.

I definitely remember feeling anxious, wondering how much of the twenty-first century I would get to see. I also recollect calming myself with the thought that "it's a long way off, no need to think about it now." Well, in spite of all my resistance, that day has arrived. On October 9 (1999)—the same birthday as the late Beatle John Lennon—I will have reached the half-century mark.

Of course, as a baby-boomer, I do not marvel alone. Everywhere, it seems, I encounter signs of interest in or concern for our now-middle-aged cohorts (leading me to wonder if all the major magazine editors gather at some private resort to plan the season's issues and headlines).

A September issue of *The Economist* demands "Let Old Folk Work!"— its cover bearing a black-and-white photo of a white-haired gent yelling into a telephone as if it's the old folks themselves demanding a return to field and factory (notably, the phone itself is an old corded model). At the same time, *Business Week*'s cover shouts "BRAIN DRAIN: With older executives set to leave the workplace in droves, Corporate America is facing a dramatic talent shortage," the accompanying picture showing another white-haired gent, this time seated in a lush leather chair, fading away from his shoes up.

The very same week, the on-line magazine *Intellectual Capital*—no doubt edited and authored by hip and ironically attuned "30-somethings" and "Gen Xers"—has dedicated an issue to "ELDERLY NATION? The

---

Originally published in *The Times Higher Education Supplement*, November 5, 1999.

baby boom will soon become the elder boom. A look at the implications." Its articles include "The Graying of the Developed Economies," "Preparing for an Aging Society," "Modern Maturity," and "The Politics of Aging"—leading me to wonder, as well, if my generation will rediscover its radicalism as we rediscover the freedom in pensioned and penurious maturity that we enjoyed at university.

There's no escaping the discourse. *The Chronicle of Higher Education* kicks off the new academic year with "The Graying Professoriate," an article that examines *The American College Teacher*, a new report on academic life by the UCLA Higher Education Research Institute. Based on surveys of almost 34,000 faculty nationwide, the report addresses teaching and research practices, technology and Internet use, professional understandings and values, campus climate and job satisfaction, and political preferences. Yet the feature of the report that receives the greatest notice is the aging of the professorial ranks. A third of U.S. faculty are now 55 or older, and in the past 10 years the percentage of university teachers and scholars under the age of 45 has fallen from 41 to 34.

I cannot help but compare my own activities and attitudes to those reported of my colleagues. The only place where I find myself truly deviating from the norm is in "political orientation." American academics generally profess center-left political views (less than 1 percent identify themselves as far right, 18 percent as conservative, 37 percent as middle-of-the-road, 40 percent as liberal, and 5 percent far left). I would have replied "far left," assuming it meant radical-democratic or socialist.

Reflecting the state of Wisconsin's budgetary ups and downs, and the pattern of new faculty recruitment afforded, three "generations" have constituted the history of my own department (generally recognized as the most left and contentious bunch on campus). Roughly speaking: The eldest generation, now retired, were liberals whose politics apparently had been shaped in the 1950s. My own now-middle-aged coterie has professed various leftist politics and persuasions, including environmentalism, feminism, and democratic socialism. And the younger folk, currently in their 30s, have generally subscribed to liberalism, but a liberalism very much attuned to feminism and multiculturalism. I sensed a generation gap when one of our junior colleagues said to me a few years back, rather defensively, but emphatically: "I am just not as *left* as the rest of you." Fair enough, I thought. As the youngest of my cohorts, I personally find lunchtime discussions of retirement plans much more bothersome than political differences.

All the talk of aging makes me ever more conscious of the "generation gap" I face every time I enter the classroom. Looking around the lecture hall of my first-year course, I realize my students have parents my age and some, possibly, grandparents not much older. What crosses their 18-year-old minds when they hear me talk about the Cold War, the 1960s, and the rise of Reaganism as part of my contemporary experience? I can tell you what often crosses mine. In the midst of recounting an experience of youth, it suddenly dawns on me that I am talking about events of about 35 years ago, leading me to blurt out: "Can I be that old? How can I possibly be talking of things that happened that many years ago?"—instigating one student to kindly ask, "Don't you get bored teaching the same courses every year?"

Occasionally, I get to share such sensations with my peers. At a recent political-studies conference a graduate student referred to himself as having been born "postwar," leading the baby-boomers present to look at each other in wonder, until we realized he meant post-Vietnam. Then our wonder turned to upset, as we realized both how old we had become and that we have no generational monopoly on the term.

To avoid completely freaking out, I continually turn to history; though, oddly enough, I found it a bit eerie when the *American Historical Review* recently published an article on the development of shopping malls in the 1950s featuring the Garden State Plaza in Paramus, New Jersey, where I grew up.[1] My generation has been widely written about, but somehow a study of my hometown and the places I haunted as a teenager seem too close and intimate to be treated as social history.

Actually, I get a kick out of telling my students that it would take only five of me, laid head-to-toe chronologically, to reach back to the eighteenth century. There, I say, you would find a young man caught up in the American Revolution or, sticking to my own family lineage, struggling to provide for a family in a Russian-Jewish *shtetl* as an artisan or tradesman.

I thereby hope to get them to appreciate the radical character of modern history and, at the same time, how intimately connected to the past we remain. Without conceding anything to the conservative Edmund Burke, and genes aside, I want them to appreciate that, for all the apparent newness of the world, we stand not so very far removed from our ancestors. Indeed, avoiding mysticism and spirituality, I ask my students if they ever hear their (absent) parents speaking to them at decision-making moments. When they admit to hearing such voices, I tell them—drawing on my own personal experience—the day will come when they will sense themselves *becoming* their parents.

Of course, young people like to think of themselves as truly original and autonomous folk. So, the last thing they probably want to consider is how their lives are permeated with historical residue. But, as I explain, such things might also serve to empower them. It gives me hope to think so.

Chapter 34

THE DIALECTIC OF MENTORING

Before departing Ithaca for the Trojan Wars, Odysseus wisely entrusted his household to his old friend, Mentor. And Mentor honorably served his long-absent king. He confronted those who occupied Odysseus' home, who spent his wealth and pursued his wife, and he chastised his fellow citizens for tolerating such criminal and immoral acts. Though he angered many, his integrity and courage did not go unappreciated. Recognizing the esteem and trust in which his wards held him, the goddess Athena presented herself in Mentor's likeness whenever she sought to advise or inspire those mortals she wished to help.

Study of the classics has declined, but the practice to which Mentor gives his name apparently thrives. Do-gooders, public officials, entertainers, and entrepreneurs celebrate and promote mentoring for everything from combating drugs to advancing corporate interests. Would-be mentors establish organizations and institutes, and write (silly) books like *Spiritual Mentoring*, *The Marriage Mentor Manual*, *The Art of Mentoring*, and *The Mentor: 15 Keys to Success in Sales, Business and Life*. Others, in volumes like Marian Wright Edelman's *Lanterns: A Memoir of Mentors*, register debts and proffer testimonials intended to encourage their fellow Americans to actively mentor the young.[1]

Young academics can turn to Clay Schoenfeld's *Mentor in a Manual: Climbing the Academic Ladder to Tenure* or Emily Toth's *Ms. Mentor's Impeccable Advice for Women in Academia* (in fact, *The Chronicle of Higher Education* offers Ms. Mentor on its on-line Career Network). Even *Radical History Review* devoted a recent issue to the subject of mentoring.[2]

It may simply be the fact that mentoring has emerged as the latest buzzword. Or it may be because my first child, Rhiannon, is a sophomore at the University of Virginia and I anxiously hope that one of her professors recognizes her potential and takes her under his or her wing. Or it may even be that, having recently turned 50, I have become more sensitive to

---

Originally appeared in *The Chronicle of Higher Education*, April 21, 2000.

matters generational. Whatever the reason, I find myself more reflective and self-conscious about my own role as a mentor.

Increasingly, I appreciate the dialectical character of the relationship. Indeed—though I would hate to give them swelled heads—I have come to recognize just how much my own development has depended on those whom I have mentored.

Of course, the academic calling has always been about mentoring. In *The Dons: Mentors, Eccentrics, and Geniuses*, Noel Annan recounts the powerful influence Oxbridge teachers had in shaping generations of British elites.[3] Although the English term "don" does not derive from the Mafia, it does hint at the patronage system we now retrospectively exalt as "mentoring." It wasn't so long ago, after all, that the old-boy system ruled American higher education. Today, such old-boy networks have survived feminism and affirmative action by admitting girls to their ranks.

Moreover, for better or worse, universities now regularly institutionalize the mentoring of new students and faculty members in formal programs. I say "for better or worse" because my one official effort—mentoring a junior faculty member—ended rather disappointingly. I was paired with someone whose personality contrasted sharply with my own. Rather reserved, my "mentee" must have found my exuberant style overbearing. I strongly encouraged him in his scholarship and even tried, unsuccessfully, to convince him to be chair of our department. He did go on to win tenure, but soon after, to my regret, he requested transfer to another department.

My own experience as a history undergraduate in the late 1960s did little to prepare me for mentoring students. The closest anyone at Rutgers came to playing that role in my career was a professor of Spanish—and he did so by sending me away, as the guinea pig for a program that Rutgers was setting up at the National Autonomous University of Mexico. I readily acknowledge what my graduate professors did for me at the University of London and Louisiana State University. But I would better describe them as offensive linemen than as mentors, for they mostly served to guard me against conservative tacklers as I headed intellectually leftward.

Like many of my generation, I entered academe hoping to advance America's democratic impulse through my scholarship and teaching. I definitely included in that aspiration the mentoring of young intellects. But, as a 28-year-old New York Jewish boy, coming from an all-male "public Ivy" college, and possessed of radical ideas, I had a lot to learn when I became a faculty member at the University of Wisconsin–Green Bay.

I naively figured my students would be pretty much like my friends and I had been. However, most of my students were women, the first generation in their families to attend college. Half were well into their 20s (making them my peers). Quite a few had family responsibilities. And—

imbued with a strong work ethic by their working- and lower-middle-class families—many labored long hours at jobs rather than borrow to pay for college.

Moreover, the majority of these Upper Midwesterners, men and women, found my aggressive, argumentative (call it Talmudic?) pedagogical style rather intimidating. Not to mention the fact that, by the late 1970s, radicalism had waned. I admired the soundly democratic bearing of my students (remember, the Green Bay Packers are a community-owned football team), but I was uncomfortable with their reticence, variously interpreting it as fear of me, respect, or plain lack of interest.

Institutional developments also inhibited mentoring relationships. The Wisconsin legislature had created the Green Bay campus in 1965 and designed it to be the innovative, interdisciplinary component of the University of Wisconsin system. Originally well financed, it had suffered serious budget cuts by the time I arrived in 1978—and it has continued to do so. Twenty-two years later, we have the same number of faculty and twice the number of students as when I started. With seven classes per year, up to 200 students each semester in my introductory course alone, and no graduate assistants (plus scholarly, community, and familial obligations), I have had only so much time to devote to individual students.

Nevertheless, irrepressible and irresistible students tend to come a professor's way. Fortunately, since my colleagues and I have varied interests and characters, we tend to find different students intriguing. Personally, I respond to the more vocal, enthusiastic, and passionate types.

Some students walk right up and demand my attention. In my first year at the university, Michael Zilles waylaid me in the hall to insist we read Marx's work together. He was brilliant (far smarter than I) and, in spite of his attraction to philosophy, we became good friends, working closely until he and his wife went off to Boston for graduate school (forcing my wife and me to find new babysitters). I had read Marx before, but probably never so carefully as I did with Michael.

Other students, whether they intended it or not, have recruited me to their cause by persistently challenging me in class and remaining undaunted in the ensuing exchanges. Scott Hoffman, a working-class "kid" whose questions revealed remarkable critical powers but whose writing needed disciplining (and got it), kept his student comrades and me forever on our toes, occasionally exasperatingly so. He incessantly asked questions about logic and theory, in response to which I pressed him to think historically. I made it a point of meeting with him after class, not sending him away—that is, until graduation, when I proudly packed him off to follow in my footsteps in pursuit of a master's degree at the London School of Economics.

Similarly, I adored Ron Sexton. He repeatedly jumped into courses over his head. Yet he pushed himself to master them, and always did eventually. We talked endlessly about the latest books and articles and, after graduation, he headed off to New York to work with labor unions, study for a graduate degree in library sciences at Columbia University, and secure appointment as chief librarian at the Carnegie Endowment.

This past fall (1999), freshman biology student Mike Halberg reminded me that Midwesterners can tangle with ideas and professors as well any East Coaster. He also made me think about how terribly foolish I must sound each year when, before the start of autumn classes, I whine to my family that all the best students have graduated. Knowing he had a medical career in mind, I refrained from trying to get him to shift to history or social science. But one day, after class, contesting my view of the historical prospects for greater equality, he so got under my skin that I shot back: "How'd you like to really develop that intellect of yours?" (More honestly, I probably should have asked him how he'd like to spend the next few years cultivating *my* intellect.) Still pre-med (I'd have it no other way), Mike works independently with me this semester, and every Thursday, over dinner in the University Commons, we grapple with the "Age of Revolution," past and present.

I would love working with graduate students; yet I know that, being an undergraduate teacher, I don't have to feel guilty about pursuing the pleasures of intellectual nomadism but can range over a variety of topics and areas (and I don't have to agonize over the academic job market). My best students have inspired me and helped prepare me for the classroom by making me explain myself more clearly before I face their more reserved comrades. They also have pushed me in new directions.

Back in the 1980s, before we hired a professor of women's history, feminist students motivated me to read the growing corpus of scholarship with them. Other students picked up my interest in the British Marxist historians and cajoled me into reading English cultural studies (though I abjured postmodernism). And just last semester, Carrie Cole, Tania Krall, and Annette Spakowicz persuaded me to tutor them on Marx, Weber, and Durkheim. Doing so, they not only gave me another chance to reconsider Durkheim, and scorn Weber, but also to more deeply appreciate Marx's dictum that "even the educators need to be educated."

NOTES

Introduction

1. In particular, see C. Wright Mills, *The Sociological Imagination* (New York: Oxford University Press, 1959). I have discussed Mills's arguments in "Redeeming Reason and Freedom: The Challenge of C. Wright Mills," in Harvey J. Kaye, *"Why Do Ruling Classes Fear History?" and Other Questions* (New York: St. Martin's Press, 1996), pp. 193–98.
2. Francis Fukuyama, "The End of History?", *The National Interest*, no. 16, Summer 1989, pp. 3–18, and *The End of History and the Last Man* (New York: Free Press, 1992). For my own review of Fukuyama's work, see "The End of History? . . . Not!", in Kaye, *"Why Do Ruling Classes Fear History?" and Other Questions*, pp. 41–50.
3. See Mari Jo Buhle, Paul Buhle, and Harvey J. Kaye, eds., *The American Radical* (New York: Routledge, 1994); and Eric Foner, *The Story of American Freedom* (New York: Norton, 1998).
4. Along with *The Times Educational Supplement* (TES) and *The Times Literary Supplement* (TLS), *The Times Higher Education Supplement* is one of three weekly newspapers published by *The Times of London*. In the first year of my commission, I contributed to World View on a quarterly basis and, thereafter, bimonthly.
5. In 1997 the London-based *Index on Censorship*, an international human rights magazine, invited me to write "U. S. Notebook." That same year, *Democratic Left*, the magazine of the Democratic Socialists of America, commissioned me to contribute a quarterly "conservative watch" column, which I titled "It's a Dirty Job, But . . ." (discussed here in Chapter 15). And in January 2000, I received an invitation to write as a columnist for *The Chronicle of Higher Education*. The first of those pieces, "The Dialectic of Mentoring," I include here as the final chapter.
6. Harvey J. Kaye, *The British Marxist Historians* (New York: St. Martin's Press, 1984, 1995 rev. ed.) and *The Education of Desire: Marxists and the Writing of History* (New York: Routledge, 1992). Also, see Chapter 21 of the present work.
7. Harvey J. Kaye, *The Powers of the Past: Reflections on the Crisis and Promise of History* (Minneapolis: University of Minnesota Press, 1991).
8. See various chapters of Kaye, *"Why Do Ruling Classes Fear History?" and Other Questions*.
9. See Harvey J. Kaye, *Thomas Paine: Firebrand of the Revolution* (New York: Oxford University Press, 2000), a young adult biography.

Chapter 1

1. Ronald Thiemann, *Religion in Public Life* (Washington, DC: Georgetown University Press, 1996).
2. Isaac Kramnick and R. Laurence Moore, *The Godless Constitution* (New York: Norton, 1996).
3. Ralph Reed, *Politically Incorrect* (Dallas: Word Books, 1994), *Contract with the American Family* (Nashville: Moorings, 1995), and *Active Faith* (New York: Free Press, 1996).
4. William J. Bennett, ed., *The Book of Virtues* (New York: Simon & Schuster, 1993) and *The Children's Book of Virtues* (New York: Simon & Schuster, 1994).
5. Amy Waldman, "Why We Need a Religious Left," *Washington Monthly*, vol. 27, no. 12, December 1995, pp. 37–43; Harvey Cox, "The Transcendent Dimension," *The Nation*, January 1, 1996, pp. 20–23; Michael Lerner, *Jewish Renewal* (New York: Putnam, 1994); Jim Wallis, *The Soul of Politics* (New York: New Press, 1994); and Cornel West, *Keeping Faith* (New York: Routledge, 1994).
6. George M. Marsden, *The Soul of the American University* (New York: Oxford University Press, 1996); Warren Nord, *Religion and American Education* (Chapel Hill: University of North Carolina Press, 1995); Mark Schwehn, *Exiles from Eden* (New York: Oxford University Press, 1992); and Alan Wolfe, "Higher Learning," *Lingua Franca*, vol. 6, no. 3, March/April 1996, pp. 70–81.
7. *Rolling Stone*, March 21, 1996.

Chapter 2

1. Christopher Lasch, *The Revolt of the Elites* (New York: Norton, 1995).
2. Kevin Phillips, *The Politics of Rich and Poor* (New York: Random House, 1990).
3. Dinesh D'Souza, *Illiberal Education* (New York: Free Press, 1987).
4. Louis Uchitelle et al., "The Downsizing of America," *The New York Times*, March 3–9, 1996, collected in *Downsizing in America* (New York: New York Times Books, 1996); and Steven Pearlstein, "The Rich Get Richer and . . .", *Washington Post (National Weekly Edition)*, June 12–18, pp. 6–7.
5. Edward Wolff, *Top Heavy* (New York: New Press, 1995); David Gordon, *Fat and Mean* (New York: Free Press, 1996); *The American Enterprise*, vol. 7, no. 4, July/August 1996; Aaron Bernstein, "The Wage Squeeze," vol. 7, no. 4, July/August 1996; Aaron Bernstein, "The Wage Squeeze," *Business Week*, July 17, 1995, pp. 55–56.
6. S. M. Miller and Karen Marie Feroggiaro, "Class Dismissed?", *American Prospect*, no. 21, Spring 1995, pp. 100–104; Sean Reilly, "The Case for Unions," *Washington Monthly*, vol. 27, nos. 7–8, July/August 1995, pp. 26–31; and Ethan Kapstein, "Workers and the World Economy," *Foreign Affairs*, vol. 75, no. 3, May/June 1996, pp. 16–37 [later Kapstein turned the piece into a book: *Sharing the Wealth: Workers and World Economy* (New York: Norton, 1999)].
7. E. J. Dionne, *They Only Look Dead* (New York: Simon & Schuster, 1996); Michael Lind, *The Next American Nation* (New York: Free Press, 1994); Kevin

Phillips, *Boiling Point* (New York: HarperCollins, 1995); and Jacob Weisberg, *In Defense of Government* (New York: Scribners, 1996).

Chapter 4

1. Robert D. Putnam, "Bowling Alone," *Journal of Democracy*, vol. 6, January 1995, pp. 65–78; E. J. Dionne, *Why Americans Hate Politics* (New York: Simon & Schuster, 1994); William Greider, *Who Will Tell the People?* (New York: Simon & Schuster, 1993); Lewis Lapham, *The Wish for Kings* (New York: Grove Press, 1993); and Jean Bethke Elshtain, *Democracy on Trial* (New York: Basic Books, 1996).
2. *Dollars and Sense*, no. 206, July/August 1996; and *The New Republic*, September 30, 1996.
3. Michael Crozier, Samuel Huntington, and Joji Watanuki, *Crisis of Democracy* (New York: NYU Press, 1995); and Francis Fukuyama, *The End of History and the Last Man* (New York: Free Press, 1992).
4. Robert Bork, *Slouching Towards Gomorrah* (New York: Regan Books, 1996).

Chapter 6

1. Lawrence Halprin, designer, *The Franklin Delano Roosevelt Memorial* (San Francisco: Chronicle Books, 1997).
2. For a new history of the period, see David M. Kennedy, *Freedom from Fear: The United States, 1929–1945* (New York: Oxford University Press, 1999).

Chapter 7

1. John Sweeney, *America Needs a Raise* (New York: Houghton Mifflin, 1996).
2. For the proceedings, see Steve Fraser and Joshua Freeman, eds., *Audacious Democracy* (New York: Houghton Mifflin, 1997).
3. Michael Denning, *The Cultural Front* (New York: Verso, 1997); and Peter Levy, *The New Left and Labor in the 1960s* (Urbana: University of Illinois Press, 1994).
4. Russell Jacoby, *The Last Intellectuals* (New York: Farrar, Straus & Giroux, 1987).
5. Max Green, *Epitaph for Labor* (Washington, DC: AEI Press, 1997).
6. Daniel Nelson, "What Happened to Organized Labor," *American Heritage*, July/August 1999, pp. 81–88.

Chapter 8

1. On the politics of the New Right, see Sara Diamond, *Roads to Dominion: Right-Wing Movements and Political Power in the United States* (New York: Guilford, 1995). On the New Right's war against the postwar liberal "social contract," see Frances Fox Piven and Richard Cloward, *The Breaking of the American Social Compact* (New York: New Press, 1997). On the New Right's use and abuse of history, see Harvey J. Kaye, *The Powers of the Past* (Minneapolis: University of Minnesota

Press, 1991); and Mike Wallace, *Mickey Mouse History and Other Essays on American Memory* (Philadelphia: Temple University Press, 1996). On the battles surrounding the national standards for history, see Gary Nash, Charlotte Crabtree, and Ross Dunn, *History on Trial: Culture Wars and the Teaching of the Past* (New York: Knopf, 1997). On the culture wars over "the past," see Edward Linenthal and Tom Engelhardt, eds., *History Wars: The Enola Gay and Other Battles for the American Past* (New York: Metropolitan Books, 1996). On the aspirations to resurrect the labor movement, see John Sweeney, *America Needs a Raise* (New York: Houghton Mifflin, 1996). On America's radical-democratic tradition, see Mari Jo Buhle, Paul Buhle, and Harvey J. Kaye, eds., *The American Radical* (New York: Routledge, 1994)—and don't fail to listen to Paul Robeson's performance of *Ballad for Americans* by Earl Robinson and John Latouche (Vanguard Records, 1989 rerelease).

Chapter 9

1. Marvin Cetron and Owen Davies, *Probable Futures: How Science and Technology Will Transform Our Lives in the Next Twenty Years* (New York: St. Martin's Press, 1997).
2. Roberto Unger and Cornel West, *The Future of American Progressivism: An Invitation for Political and Economic Reform* (Boston: Beacon, 1997).
3. Russell Jacoby, *The End of Utopia: Politics and Culture in an Age of Apathy* (New York: Basic Books, 1999).
4. John Gray, *False Dawn* (New York: New Press, 1998); and George Soros, *The Crisis of Global Capitalism* (New York: Public Affairs, 1998).
5. Russell Jacoby, *The Last Intellectuals* (New York: Farrar, Straus & Giroux, 1987).
6. Russell Jacoby, *Dogmatic Wisdom* (New York: Doubleday, 1994).
7. Todd Gitlin, *The Twilight of Common Dreams* (New York: Owl, 1996 reprint edition); and Richard Rorty, *Achieving Our Country* (Cambridge, MA: Harvard University Press, 1997).

Chapter 10

1. Eric Hobsbawm and Marc Weitzmann, *1968: Magnum Throughout the World* (Paris: Hazan, 1998); and Tariq Ali and Susan Watkins, *1968: Marching in the Streets* (New York: Free Press, 1998).
2. Christopher Hitchens, "The Children of '68," *Vanity Fair*, June 1998, pp. 92–103.

Chapter 11

1. Karl Marx and Friedrich Engels, *The Communist Manifesto*, with an Introduction by Ellen Meiksins Wood (New York: Monthly Review Press, 1998 edition).
2. Kim Moody, *Workers in a Lean World* (New York: Verso, 1997).
3. *Weekly Standard*, "Is There a Worldwide Conservative Crack-Up? A Symposium," August 25/September 1, 1997.

Chapter 12

1. Anthony Giddens, *Capitalism and Modern Social Theory* (New York: Cambridge University Press, 1971).
2. Anthony Giddens, *Beyond Left and Right: The Future of Radical Politics* (Cambridge, UK: Polity Press, 1994).
3. Anthony Giddens, *The Third Way: The Renewal of Social Democracy* (Cambridge, UK: Polity Press, 1998).
4. T. H. Marshall, *Citizenship and Social Class* (New York: Cambridge University Press, 1950).
5. Daniel Singer, *Whose Millennium? Theirs or Ours?* (New York: Monthly Review Press, 1999).

Chapter 13

1. "Revolutionary War Symbol, the Liberty Tree, Is Cut Down," *The New York Times*, October 26, 1999, p. A20.
2. Benjamin Barber, *An Aristocracy of Everyone* (New York: Ballantine, 1992), p. 30; and Joyce Appleby, Lynn Hunt, and Margaret Jacob, *Telling the Truth About History* (New York: Norton, 1994), p. 236.
3. Harvey J. Kaye, *The Powers of the Past* (Minneapolis: University of Minnesota Press, 1991) and "Whose History Is It?", *Monthly Review*, vol. 48, no. 6, November 1996, pp. 16–30; and Gary B. Nash, Charlotte Crabtree, and Ross E. Dunn, *History on Trial: Culture Wars and the Teaching of the Past* (New York: Knopf, 1997).
4. Herbert Gutman, "Whatever Happened to History?", *The Nation*, November 21, 1981, pp. 553–54; Nathan Huggins, *Revelations: American History, American Myths* (New York: Oxford University Press, 1995), p. 127; Sara Evans, *Born for Liberty: A History of Women in America* (New York: Free Press, 1989), p. 2; and Appleby, Hunt, and Jacob, *Telling the Truth About History*, p. 235.
5. Martin E. Marty, *The One and the Many* (Cambridge, MA: Harvard University Press, 1997); Robert Pinsky, "Poetry and American Memory," *Atlantic Monthly*, October 1999, pp. 60–70; and Andrew Delbanco, *The Real American Dream* (Cambridge, MA: Harvard University Press, 1999).
6. Jeff Faux, *The Party's Not Over* (New York: Basic Books, 1996); Michael Lind, "The Liberal Search for a Usable Past," *The New Leader*, April 6–20, 1998, pp. 11–13, and *The Next American Nation* (New York: Free Press, 1994); Sean Prigo, "Soul Searching in the Arizona Desert," *Insight Magazine*, February 1, 1999, pp. 18–19; and Steve Darnall and Alex Ross, *U.S.* (New York: D.C./Vertigo Comics, 1997).
7. Roy Rosenzweig and David Thelen, *The Presence of the Past* (New York: Columbia University Press, 1998), especially Chapter 5, "Beyond the Intimate Past," pp. 115–46.
8. Nathan Glazer, "American Epic: Then and Now," *The Public Interest*, no. 130, Winter 1998, pp. 3–20.

9. Arthur Schlesinger, Jr., *The Disuniting of America* (New York: Norton, 1992).

10. American Social History Project, *Who Built America?*, 2 volumes (New York: Pantheon, 1989 and 1992); Ronald Takaki, *A Different Mirror* (Boston: Little, Brown, 1993); and Eric Foner, *The Story of American Freedom* (New York: Norton, 1998).

11. The Post-Modernity Project of the University of Virginia (fieldwork conducted by the Gallup Poll Organization, Inc.), *The State of Disunion: 1996 Survey of American Political Culture* (Charlottesville, VA, 1996). Rosenzweig and Thelen also report that their respondents want a narrative of the civic heritage taught to their children in favor of active citizenship and taking "responsibility for maintaining freedom and democracy" (*The Presence of the Past*, p. 194).

12. Joy Hakim, *A History of US* (New York: Oxford University Press, 1999 rev. ed.). On Hakim's work compared to standard textbooks, see Alexander Stille, "The Betrayal of History," *New York Review of Books*, June 11, 1998, pp. 15–20.

13. *Life Magazine*, special Spring 1997 issue. On the American radical tradition, see Mari Jo Buhle, Paul Buhle, and Harvey J. Kaye, eds., *The American Radical* (New York: Routledge, 1994).

14. The Post-Modernity Project, *The State of Disunion*, p. 17.

15. "After 30 Years, the Nation's Living Symbol Is Deemed Safe," *The New York Times*, July 3, 1999, p. A8; and Irvin Molotsky, "New Dawn for Flag That Was Still There," *The New York Times*, May 25, 1999, p. D5.

Chapter 15

1. Harvey J. Kaye, *The British Marxist Historians* (New York: St. Martin's Press, 1995 new edition) and *The Education of Desire: Marxists and the Writing of History* (New York: Routledge, 1992). Also, see Chapter 21 of the present work.

2. Harvey J. Kaye, *The Powers of the Past* (Minneapolis: University of Minnesota Press, 1991).

3. On the American punditocracy, see Eric Alterman, *Sound and Fury: The Washington Punditocracy and the Collapse of American Politics* (Ithaca, NY: Cornell University Press, 1999 rev. ed.).

4. See Richard J. Neuhaus, ed., *The End of Democracy?* (Dallas: Spence, 1997), for a collection of the contributions to the symposium and diverse conservatives' reactions to it.

5. Harvey J. Kaye, *"Why Do Ruling Classes Fear History?" and Other Questions* (New York: St. Martin's Press, 1996).

6. David Brooks, "A Return to National Greatness," *Weekly Standard*, March 3, 1997, 16–21.

Chapter 17

1. See Richard J. Neuhas, ed., *The End of Democracy?* (Dallas: Spence, 1997); Mitchell S. Muncy, *The End of Democracy? II* (Dallas: Spence, 1999); and Jim Wallis, *Who Speaks for God?* (New York: Delacorte, 1996).

2. Donald Barlett and James Steele, *America, What Went Wrong?* (Kansas City: Andrews McMeel, 1992) and *America, Who Stole the Dream?* (Kansas City: Andrews McMeel, 1996); G. William Domhoff, *Who Rules America?* (Mountain View, CA: Mayfield, 1998); Harvey Jacobs, ed., *Who Owns America?* (Madison: University of Wisconsin Press, 1998); William Greider, *Who Will Tell the People?* (New York; Simon & Schuster, 1992); and Eric Alterman, *Who Speaks for America?* (Ithaca, NY: Cornell University Press, 1998).

3. Byron Shafer, ed., *Is America Different?* (Oxford: Clarendon, 1991); Graham Wilson, *Only in America?* (New York: Chatham House, 1998); and Richard Etulain, ed., *Does the Frontier Make America Exceptional?* (Boston: Bedford, 1999).

4. Michael Lind, *The Next American Nation* (New York: Free Press, 1995).

5. David Batstone and Eduardo Mendieta, eds., *The Good Citizen* (New York: Routledge, 1999); and John Hall and Charles Lindholm, *Is America Breaking Apart?* (Princeton, NJ: Princeton University Press, 1999).

6. Gregory Pence, *Who's Afraid of Human Cloning?* (Lanham, MD: Rowman & Littlefield, 1998).

Chapter 18

1. Hilton Kramer and Roger Kimball, *The Future of the European Past* (Chicago: I. A. Dee, 1997).

Chapter 19

1. Howard Zinn, *The Zinn Reader* (New York: Seven Stories Press, 1997).

2. For John Silber's own reflections, see "Procedure or Dogma: The Core of Liberalism," *New Criterion*, May 1999, pp. 4–12.

3. Howard Zinn, *You Can't Be Neutral on a Moving Train* (Boston: Beacon, 1994).

4. Howard Zinn, *LaGuardia in Congress* (Ithaca, NY: Cornell University Press, 1959).

5. Howard Zinn, *A People's History of the United States* (New York: New Press, 1997 teaching edition).

6. Martin Shaw, "From Total War to Democratic Peace: Peace, Exterminism and Historical Pacifism," in Harvey J. Kaye and Keith McClelland, eds., *E. P. Thompson: Critical Perspectives* (Philadelphia: Temple University Press, 1990), pp. 233–51.

Chapter 20

1. Doug Stewart, "This Joint Is Jumping," *Smithsonian*, vol. 29, no. 12, March 1999, pp. 60–77; Tom Brokaw, *The Greatest Generation* (New York: Random House, 1998); and Stephen E. Ambrose, *Citizen Soldiers* (New York: Simon & Schuster, 1997).

2. Brokaw, *The Greatest Generation*, pp. xix, xxiii–xxvi, xxx. On Spielberg, see Stephen J. Dubner, "Steven the Good," *The New York Times Magazine*, February 14, 1999, pp. 38–75.

3. Here's how it happened: One day in September 1980, my father received a copy of the 11th Armored veterans' magazine that included a short piece by a fellow named Eli Warach. It came as quite a surprise. Warach, a lieutenant, had rescued my dad after his tank had been hit, but they had had no contact since then. In fact, each assumed the other was killed in battle. Not only were both still alive, but they lived only 15 minutes away from each other in northern New Jersey. Seeing Warach's name, my father immediately looked up the phone number and called him. When Warach answered, my father asked, "Do you remember January 1st, 1944?" Warach shot back with a laugh, "It was 1945, you dope. This must be Murray Kaye!" They wanted to celebrate and, as both were Jewish, they arranged to get together with their wives at the end of the High Holy Days, that is, to break the fast of Yom Kippur together. The two couples became dear friends, and they made breaking the fast an annual tradition until my father's death in 1990. Warach, who worked in publishing, had related the story to Mike Kelly, a columnist at *The Record*, the leading newspaper of northern New Jersey. Kelly recounted it in a piece he titled "To Life" (October 8, 1989).

4. Charles B. MacDonald, *A Time for Trumpets: The Untold Story of the Battle of the Bulge* (New York: William Morrow, 1985); and Michael Green and Gladys Green, *Patton and the Battle of the Bulge* (Osceola, WI: MBI Publishing, 1999).

Chapter 21

1. Francois Furet, *The Passing of an Illusion*, translated by Deborah Furet (University of Chicago Press, 1999), pp. 502–3; and Francis Fukuyama, *The End of History and the Last Man* (New York: Free Press, 1992). For radically different views of socialist and democratic possibilities, see Daniel Singer, *Whose Millennium? Theirs or Ours?* (New York: Monthly Review Press, 1999); and Pierre Bourdieu, *Acts of Resistance: Against the Tyranny of the Market* (New York: New Press, 1999).

2. Harvey J. Kaye, *The Powers of the Past* (Minneapolis: University of Minnesota Press, 1991) and *"Why Do Ruling Classes Fear History?" and Other Questions* (New York: St. Martin's Press, 1996).

3. Walter Benjamin, "Theses in the Philosophy of History," in his *Illuminations* (New York: Harcourt Brace, 1969), p. 255.

4. Harvey J. Kaye, *The British Marxist Historians* (New York: St. Martin's Press, 1984, 1995 rev. ed.) and *The Education of Desire* (New York: Routledge, 1992).

5. Maurice Dobb, *Studies in the Development of Capitalism* (London: Routledge & Kegan Paul, 1946). The book instigated a vibrant debate on the question of the transition, reaching well beyond the Historians' Group. See Rodney Hilton, ed., *The Transition from Feudalism to Capitalism* (London: Verso, 1976).

6. On the Hammonds and Webbs as labor historians, see David Sutton, "Radical Liberalism, Fabianism, and Social History," in R. Johnson et al., eds., *Making Histories* (London: Hutchinson, 1982), pp. 15–43. For an example of Cole's work, see G. D. H. Cole and R. Postgate, *The Common People, 1746–1946* (London: Methuen, 1946 rev. ed.).

7. A. L. Morton, *A People's History of England* (London: Lawrence & Wishart, 1938, 1979 rev. ed.).

8. Torr edited *Karl Marx and Friedrich Engels, Correspondence 1846–1895* (London: Lawrence, 1934) and authored *Tom Mann and His Times* (London: Lawrence & Wishart, 1956). For a sampler of work produced by the Group in honor of Torr, see John Saville, ed., *Democracy and the Labour Movement* (London: Lawrence & Wishart, 1954).

9. For example, see E. P. Thompson, ed., *Out of Apathy* (London: Stevens, 1960); and Thompson, *The Poverty of Theory and Other Essays* (London: Merlin Press, 1978).

10. For example: Rodney Hilton, *Bond Men Made Free* (London: Methuen, 1973), *The English Peasantry in the Later Middle Ages* (Oxford, UK: Oxford University Press, 1975), and *Class Conflict and the Crisis of Feudalism* (London: Hambledon Press, 1984); Christopher Hill, *Puritanism and Revolution* (London: Secker & Warburg, 1958), *Society and Puritanism in Pre-Revolutionary England* (London: Secker & Warburg, 1964), and *Intellectual Origins of the English Revolution* (Oxford, UK: Oxford University Press, 1965); George Rudé, *The Crowd in the French Revolution* (Oxford, UK: Oxford University Press, 1959), *Wilkes and Liberty* (Oxford, UK: Oxford University Press, 1962), *The Crowd in History* (New York: Wiley, 1964), *Captain Swing* with E. J. Hobsbawm (New York: Pantheon, 1968), and *The Face in the Crowd* edited by H. J. Kaye (London: Harvester, 1988); Eric Hobsbawm, *Primitive Rebels* (Manchester, UK: Manchester University Press, 1959), *Labouring Men* (London: Weidenfeld, 1964), and *Nations and Nationalism Since 1780* (Cambridge, UK: Cambridge University Press, 1990); E. P. Thompson, *The Making of the English Working Class* (London: Gollancz, 1963), *Whigs and Hunters* (London: Allen Lane, 1975), and *Customs in Common* (New York: New Press, 1991); John Saville, *1848: The British State and the Chartist Movement* (Cambridge, UK: Cambridge University Press, 1987) and *The Labour Movement in Britain* (London: Faber & Faber, 1988); Dorothy Thompson, *The Chartists* (New York: Pantheon, 1984); Victor Kiernan, *The Lords of Human Kind* (Harmondsworth, UK: Penguin, 1972 rev. ed.), *State and Society in Europe, 1550–1650* (Oxford: Blackwell, 1980), *European Empires from Conquest to Collapse* (New York: Pantheon, 1982), and *Imperialism and Its Contradictions* edited by H. J. Kaye (New York: Routledge, 1995). For additional bibliographical references, see Kaye, *The British Marxist Historians* and *The Education of Desire*.

11. For a rather different view of the class question, see David Cannidine, *The Rise and Fall of Class in Britain* (New York Columbia University Press, 1999). It amazes me that after a generation of Thatcherism and Reaganism—that is, vigorous class war from above—historians and social scientists have taken to eschewing the centrality of class and class conflict in the modern world.

12. Power and the powerful have been foremost subjects in the work of V. G. Kiernan, for example, *The Lords of Human Kind* (Harmondsworth, UK: Penguin, 1972 rev. ed.), *State and Society in Europe, 1550–1650* (Oxford: Blackwell, 1980), and *History Classes and Nation-States: Selected Writings of V. G. Kiernan* edited by H. J. Kaye (Oxford: Polity/Blackwell, 1988). But consider, as well, works such as Edward Thompson's *Whigs and Hunters*.

13. E. P. Thompson, *The Making of The English Working Class*, p. 12.

14. See George Rudé, *Ideology and Popular Protest* (Chapel Hill: University of North Carolina Press, 1980, 1995 rev. ed.); and Harvey J. Kaye, "Political Theory and History: Antonio Gramsci and the British Marxist Historians," in *The Education of Desire*, pp. 9–30. Also see, for example, Christopher Hill, ed., *The World Turned Upside Down* (Harmondsworth,UK: Penguin, 1972, 1975), *Winstanley, The Law of Freedom and Other Writings* (Cambridge, UK: Cambridge University Press, 1983 rev. ed.), *Milton and the English Revolution* (London: Faber, 1977), and *A Turbulent, Seditious and Factious People: John Bunyan and His Church* (London: Allen Lane, 1988); and E. P. Thompson, *William Morris: Romantic to Revolutionary* (New York: Pantheon, 1955, 1977 rev. ed.), *Persons and Polemics* (London: Merlin Press, 1994), *Witness Against the Beast: William Blake and the Moral Law* (New York: New Press, 1993), and *The Romantics* (New York: New Press, 1997); and Eric Hobsbawm, *Uncommon People* (New York: New Press, 1998).

15. Dietrich Rueschmeyer, "Capitalism," in S. M. Lipset, ed., *Encyclopedia of Democracy* (Washington: Congressional Quarterly Press, 1995), p. 2169. Also, see Dietrich Rueschmeyer, Evelyne Huber Stephens, and John Stephens, *Capitalist Development and Democracy* (Chicago: University of Chicago Press, 1993).

16. In particular, one could find the historians' essays, commentaries, and reviews in the periodicals *New Society*, *New Statesman*, *The London Review of Books*, *Tribune*, and *Marxism Today*. See David Rubinstein, ed., *People for the People* (London: Ithaca Press, 1973), for a collection of biographical and movement portraits by the historians and others that originally appeared as a series in *Tribune*.

17. See Dennis Dworkin, *Cultural Marxism in Postwar Britain* (Durham, NC: Duke University Press, 1997), especially pp. 45–125.

18. Eric Hobsbawm, *The Age of Revolution, 1789–1848* (London: Weidenfeld, 1962), *The Age of Capital, 1848–1875* (London: Weidenfeld, 1975), *The Age of Empire, 1875–1914* (London: Weidenfeld, 1987), and *The Age of Extremes, 1914–1991* (New York: Pantheon, 1995). Also, see Eric Hobsbawm, *On History* (New York: New Press, 1997), for a collection of his historiographical writings.

19. For example, see Eric Hobsbawm, *Revolutionaries* (London: Weidenfeld, 1973) and *Politics for a Rational Left* (London: Verso, 1989).

20. See Harvey J. Kaye, "E. P. Thompson, the British Marxist Historical Tradition and the Contemporary Crisis," in *The Education of Desire*, pp. 98–115. For examples of Thompson's most engaged writings, see *Writing by Candlelight* (London: Merlin Press, 1980), *Protest and Survive* with other contributors (Harmondsworth, UK: Penguin, 1980), and *The Heavy Dancers* (London: Merlin Press, 1984).

Chapter 22

1. Marc Bloch, *Strange Defeat* (New York: Norton, 1946, 1999 reprint).

2. Russell Jacoby, *The Last Intellectuals* (New York: Farrar, Straus & Giroux, 1987) and *Dogmatic Wisdom* (New York: Doubleday, 1994).

3. C. Wright Mills, *The Sociological Imagination* (New York: Oxford University Press, 1959).

Chapter 23

1. Rita Kramer, *Ed School Follies* (New York: Free Press, 1991); and Chester Finn, *We Must Take Charge* (New York: Free Press, 1991).
2. Henry Giroux, *Schooling and the Struggle for Public Life* (Minneapolis: University of Minnesota Press, 1988); and Joe Kincheloe, *Toward a Critical Politics of Teacher Thinking* (Boston: Bergin & Garvey, 1993).
3. Alison Schneider, "Taking Aim at Student Incoherence," *The Chronicle of Higher Education*, March 26, 1999, pp. A16–18.
4. Gary Smith, "Learning to Speak and Speaking to Learn," *College Teaching*, vol. 45, no. 2, Spring 1997, pp. 49–51.

Chapter 25

1. C. Wright Mills, *The Sociological Imagination* (New York: Oxford University Press, 1959).

Chapter 26

1. Todd Gitlin, *The Sixties: Years of Hope, Days of Rage* (New York: Bantam, 1993 rev. ed.); Jim Miller, *Democracy Is in the Streets* (Cambridge, MA: Harvard University Press, 1994 rev. ed.); Maurice Isserman, *If I Had a Hammer* (Urbana: University of Illinois Press, 1993 reprint ed.); Meta Mendel-Reyes, *Reclaiming Democracy* (New York: Routledge, 1996); David Farber, *The Age of Great Dreams* (New York: Hill & Wang, 1994); Kenneth Heineman, *Campus Wars* (New York: New York University Press, 1994); and Jim Farrell, *The Spirit of the Sixties* (New York: Routledge, 1997).

Chapter 29

1. On William McDonough, see "Visionary Architects" in *Time*, February 22, 1999, pp. 70–82.
2. Guy Wilson, *Thomas Jefferson's Academical Village* (Charlottesville: University of Virginia Press, 1993); and Roger Lewis, *Architect?—A Candid Guide to the Profession* (Cambridge, MA: MIT Press, 1998).
3. Karen Levin Coburn and Madge Lawrence Treeger, *Letting Go: A Parents' Guide to Today's College Experience* (New York: HarperCollins, 1997 rev. ed.).

Chapter 30

1. James Axtell, *The Pleasures of Academe* (Lincoln, NE: University of Nebraska Press, 1998).

Chapter 33

1. Lizabeth Cohen, "From Town Center to Shopping Center: The Reconfiguration of Community Marketplaces in Postwar America," *American Historical Review*, vol. 101, no. 4, October 1996, pp. 980–1081.

Chapter 34

1. Marian Wright Edelman, *Lanterns: A Memoir of Mentors* (Boston: Beacon, 1999).
2. Clay Schoenfeld, *Mentor in a Manual: Climbing the Academic Ladder to Tenure* (New York: Atwood Publishing, 1994); Emily Toth, *Ms. Mentor's Impeccable Advice for Women in Academia* (Philadelphia: University of Pennsylvania Press, 1997); and *Radical History Review*, no. 71, Spring 1998.
3. Noel Annan, *The Dons: Mentors, Eccentrics, and Geniuses* (Chicago: University of Chicago Press, 2000).

Index

Academics. *See* Professors
Addams, Jane, 59
Affirmative action, 8, 12, 35, 67
AFL-CIO, 9, 28–33, 37–38, 117, 132
African-American Studies, 58, 71
Alterman, Eric, 75
Ambrose, Stephen, 85
American Enterprise Institute (AEI), 30, 36, 67, 74
American exceptionalism, 74–76
American Historical Association (AHA), 72
American Legion, 21
American Revolution, 35, 55, 140
American University, 30
Anderson, Martin, 88
Annan, Noel, 142
Anthony, Susan B., 59
Appleby, Joyce, 56
Architecture, 26–27, 125–127
Arnold, Matthew, 43
Aronson, Ronald, 69
Australians, 118–119
Axtell, James, xi, 128

Barber, Benjamin, 56, 97
Barnes, Fred, 23
Barros, Carlos, 134–137
Benjamin, Walter, 88, 93
Bennett, William, 4–5, 36, 98
Bentham, Jeremy, 106
Blair, Tony, 51–54
Bloch, Marc, 97, 100

Bookstores, 63–65, 120
Boris, Eileen, xii, 127
Britain, xv, xviii, 51–52, 63, 78, 88–93, 118–121
British Marxist historians, ix, xv, 67, 87–93, 144
Brokaw, Tom, 83
Brooks, David, 69
Bryan, William Jennings, 76
Buchanan, Pat, 4, 9, 26, 54
Buckley, William F., Jr., 50, 67–68
Bush, George, 36, 56
Business and corporations, xvi, 4, 19–23, 28, 40, 115–116, 130
Butler, Stuart, 69

Capitalism, 19–23, 47–49, 64, 89–90
Carson, Rachel, 59
Casteen, John, 126
Center for Democratic Values, 69
Centrism ("vital center"), 11–13, 51–54
Chavez, Cesar, 29, 39, 59
Chavez-Thompson, Linda, 30
Cheney, Lynne, 36, 98
Children, 65, 71–73
Christian Coalition, 4, 68
Christian Right, 3–5, 13, 66
Chronicle of Higher Education, xii, xiv, 108, 132, 139, 141
Chronicles (Rockford Institute), 16, 68
Citizenship, xiii–xiv, 15–18, 20–21, 85–86, 97–100, 103–104
Civil rights, 9, 45, 53

157

Class and class politics, xiv, 7–10, 28, 47–50, 51–54, 89–91
Clinton, William Jefferson (Bill), 8, 11–14, 17, 26, 36, 51, 54, 56, 67, 69, 74
Cohan, George M., 79
Cold War, xiii, 49, 92–93, 140
Cole, Carrie, xi, 144
Columbia University, 29, 144
Commentary, 16, 67, 74
Community, xiii
Congress (U.S.), 8, 13, 26, 37, 76
Coniff, Ruth, 27
Conservatives and conservatism (New Right), xiv–xvii, 4–5, 7, 9, 12, 15–18, 20, 23, 26, 28, 30, 34–39, 50, 55, 58, 66–70, 83, 97–99, 101–102, 133
Constitution (U.S.), xiii, 3–4, 26
Cox, Harvey, 5
Crevecouer, Jean de, 76
Culture wars, xvi–xvii, 3–6, 15–18, 35–39, 55–60, 66–70, 98–99, 128
Cureton, Jeannette, 131

Debs, Eugene, 39
Delbanco, Andrew, 57
Democracy and democratic development, xiii–xvi, xviii, 14, 15–18, 38, 43, 49, 52–54, 55, 85, 88–93, 103
Democratic Party, 8, 10, 11–14, 24
Democratic Socialists of America (DSA), 28, 69, 145
Dickens, Charles, 46, 113
Dionne, E.J., 13, 15
Disabilities, 27
Disney Corporation, 40
Dissent, 29
Dobb, Maurice, 88–89
Douglass, Frederick, 39, 59
D'Souza, Dinesh, 8, 98
Duke University, 132
Durkheim, Emile, 52, 144

Edelman, Marian Wright, 141
Ehrenreich, Barbara, 69, 76

Elshtain, Jean Bethke, 15
Engels, Friedrich, 43, 89–91
English Revolution, 90–91
Equality and inequality, xiii, xiv, xvi, 8, 17, 53–54
Europe, 7, 26, 49, 51–52, 54, 69, 77–79, 93, 134
Evans, Sara, 56
Evergreen College (Washington), 106

Falwell, Jerry, 4
Farrell, Jim, 116
Fascism and Nazism, 26, 41, 81–82, 83–85
Feminism, 17, 139, 144
Finn, Chester, 101
First Things, 68, 74
Florescano, Enrique, 135
Foner, Eric, 29, 59
Founders (Founding Fathers), 3–4, 16, 75
France, 135–136
Fraser, Steven, xii, 29
Freedom and liberty, xiii, xiv, 27, 91
Free trade, 8
French Revolution, 7
Friedan, Betty, 29
Friendship, 69, 128–130
Fruchtman, Jack, 72
Frum, David, 69
Fukuyama, Francis, xiii–xiv, 35–36, 41, 67, 74, 88
Furet, Francois, 87–88, 93

Galt, Tony, xi, 129
Gambling, 63, 65
George Washington University, 31
Georgetown University, 132
Germany, 82, 83–85, 97
Giddens, Anthony, 51–54
Gingrich, Newt, xvii, 4, 12, 18
Giroux, Henry, xi, 102
Gitlin, Todd, 43, 116
Glazer, Nathan, 58, 67
Goldwater, Barry, 45
Gramsci, Antonio, 103

Gray, John, 41
Greece, 77
Greek mythology, 141
Green Bay (WI), 19–24, 40, 63
Green Bay Packers, ix, xi, 19–24, 143
Greider, William, 15
Gutman, Herbert, 56

Hakim, Joy, 59
Halberg, Mike, xi, 144
Halprin, Lawrence, 26–27
Hamilton, Alexander, 76
Harvard University, xvii, 3, 5, 69, 132
Healthcare, 12
Heinemann, Kenneth, 116
Heroes, 18, 59
Hein, Steve, xi, 23,
Heritage Foundation, 67, 69
Hill, Christopher, 89–93
Hilton, Rodney, 89–93
Historical education, xv, 36, 93, 98–100, 124
History and historians, xiv–xv, 4, 18, 25–27, 33–39, 48, 55–59, 66, 77–79, 80–82, 83, 86–93, 97–100, 123–124, 134–137
Hitchens, Christopher, 44–45
Hitler, Adolf, 82, 84
Hobsbawm, Eric, 44, 89–93, 135
Hoffman, Scott, 143
Holocaust, 82
Horowitz, David, 74
Huggins, Nathan, 56
Hunt, Lynn, 56
Hutton, Lauren, 112

Ideology, xv
Iggers, George, 135
Industry and industrial revolution, 89–92
Intellectuals, xiii–xiv, xviii, 4–5, 17, 25, 28–33, 38, 41–43, 53, 72, 87–93, 97–100
Interdisciplinary studies, 106–109, 122–123
Isserman, Maurice, 116

Jacoby, Russell, 29, 40–43, 98
Japanese Americans, 26
Jefferson, Thomas, 3, 11–12, 25, 59, 125–126
Jews and American Jewish culture, xvi, 5, 13, 26, 74, 80, 140, 142–143
Jobbins, David, xi, xv–xvi
Johnson, Lyndon Baines, 35, 45
Jowett, David, xi, 129–130

Kaye, Fiona, ix, 126, 134–135
Kaye, Frances (Sehres), 84
Kaye, Lorna (Stewart), ix, 120–121, 125–127, 134–135
Kaye, Murray, 84–86, 152
Kaye, Rhiannon, ix, 72, 125–127, 141
Kazin, Michael, xii, 72
Keane, John, 72
Keller, Helen, 59
Kelley, Robin, 71
Kennedy, John F., 76
Kennedy, Robert F. (Bobby), 46
Kiernan, Victor, 89–93
Kimball, Roger, 79
Kincheloe, Joe, 102
King, Martin Luther, Jr., 35, 39, 46, 59
Krall, Tania, xi, 144
Kramer, Hilton, 79
Kramer, Rita, 101
Kramnick, Isaac, xi, 3, 13
Kristol, Irving, 67, 98

La Follette, Robert, 107
Labor movement and unions, xv, xviii, 8–10, 13, 17, 25, 28–33, 49, 89–93, 117, 120, 132–133, 144
Lapham, Lewis, 15
Lasch, Christopher, 7
Lennon, John, 138
Leno, Jay, 112
Lerner, Michael, 5
Levine, Arthur, 13
Lewis, Roger, 127
Liberals and liberalism, xv, 5, 29, 41, 51–54, 139

Lichtenstein, Nelson, xii, 29, 127
Lind, Michael, 9, 57, 75
Lingua Franca, 29
Lockard, Craig, xi, 129
Lombardi, Vince, 20–22
London, 63, 65, 91, 118–121
London School of Economics (LSE), 52, 119–121, 142–143
Louisiana State University (LSU), 121, 142

McCarthy, Joseph, 23
McDonough, William, 125, 127
Marshall, T.H., 52–53
Marty, Martin E., 57
Marx, Karl, 43, 47–50, 52, 89–91, 136, 143–144
May, Elaine Tyler, 71
Media, xvii, 8, 13, 15, 20, 23, 54
Medicaid, 12
Medicare, 12
Memory (public), 26, 34–39, 49, 77–79, 83–86
Mendel-Reyes, Meta, 116
Mentoring, 140–144
Mexico, 44, 46, 135, 142
Middle class, 8–10
Miller, Jim, 116
Mills, C. Wright, xiii, 53, 114
Montgomery, David, 29
Moody, Kim, 49
Morris, Dick, 51
Morton, A.L., 88–89
Mother Jones, 29, 39, 59, 75
Multiculturalism, 41–42, 58–59, 75, 139
Murdoch, Rupert, xvii, 67
Museums, 77–79
Music, 134

Nation, 29
National Education Association (NEA), 101
National Endowment for the Humanities (NEH), 5, 13
National Football League (NFL), 19, 23

National Public Radio (NPR), 21, 44
National Review, 15–16
National Standards for History, 36
National University of Mexico, 118, 142
Nelson, Daniel, 33
New England Patriots, 19, 21–22
New York City, xvi, 63, 131, 144
New York Times, 8, 16, 20, 77, 112, 132
Nixon, Richard, 46

Osborne, Joan, 6
Oxford University, 106
Oxford University Press, 71–73

Pacificism, 81–82
Paine, Thomas, xviii, 39, 71–73, 91, 93
Paramus (NJ), 140
parent(ing), xvii, 125–127
Peasants, 90–92
Perkins, Mark, xi, 110
Perry, Tom, xi
Philips, Kevin, 8–9
Pinsky, Robert, 57
Piven, Frances Fox, ix–xi, 29
Playboy, 115–116
Polls and surveys, 74
Postmodernism, 43, 144
Professors, xviii, 17, 97–100, 108–111, 112–114, 128–130, 135–136, 139, 141–144
Progressive, The, xii, xiv, 27
Putnam, Robert D., 15

Race and racism, 9
Radical tradition and the left, xviii, 5, 37–39, 43, 54, 59, 68–69, 91, 132–133
Reagan, Ronald, xv, 7, 17, 28, 35, 49, 66–67, 140
Reed, Ralph, 4–5
Religion, 3–6, 13, 68, 75, 132
Republican Party (GOP), xv, 7–9, 11–13, 17, 24, 26, 51, 57, 117
Revel, Jacques, 135–136
Rights, 53, 91, 93
Riis, Jacob, 59

Robeson, Paul, 39
Rodesch, Jerry, xi, 129–130
Roosevelt, Eleanor, 27, 59
Roosevelt, Franklin Delano, 11, 15, 25–27, 35, 59
Rorty, Richard, 29, 43, 75
Rosenzweig, Roy, 57
Rudé, George, 89–93
Rutgers University, 45, 105, 115–117, 118–119, 126, 142

St Cloud State University (Minnesota), 113
San Francisco (CA), 63
Saville, John, 89–93
Schlesinger, Arthur, Jr., 58
Scholars, Artists and Writers for Social Justice (SAWSJ), xii, 25, 28–33, 38
Second World War, 25–26, 80–82, 83–86
Sexton, Ron, 144
Sheibley, Tom, 21
Silber, John, 80
Singer, Daniel, 53
Sixties generation, xiii, xvi, 29, 36, 44–46, 66, 85–86, 97–98, 115–117, 132, 140
Smith, Gary, 104
Social sciences, 122–124
Socialism and social democracy, xv, 37, 47–54, 69, 75, 87–93
Sojourners, 5, 33, 75
Soros, George, 41, 54
Soviet Union, xiii, 35, 82, 87–89
Spain, 134–137
Spakowicz, Annette, xi, 144
Spielberg, Stephen, 83–84
Students, xi, 99, 105, 108, 110–111, 116–117, 118–121, 123–124, 131–133, 139–140, 142–144
Susman, Warren, 105
Sweeney, John, 28–30, 32, 37–38

Takaki, Ronald, 59
Teacher education, 101–105

Teaching, xv–xviii, 98–100, 101–105, 111, 112–114, 140, 141–144
Teamsters Union, 21, 31
Tecumseh, 59
Television, 8, 20, 74
Thatcher, Margaret, xv, 3, 49–50, 53, 66–67, 78, 88
Thelen, David, 57
Thiemann, Ronald, 3
Third Way politics, 51–54
Thompson, Dorothy, 89–93
Thompson, E.P., 81, 89–93
Thompson, Tommy, 54
Tikkun, xii, xiv, 29
Times Higher Education Supplement (THES), xii, xiv–xviii, 105, 122–123
Tocqueville, Alexis de, 3–4, 15
Toff, Nancy, 71–73
Toledano, Ralph de, 26
Torr, Dona, 88–89
Trilateral Commission, 17

Universities and higher education, xv–xvii, 106–111
University College London (UCL), 106, 119–120
University of California at Berkeley, xvii, 132
University of Michigan, 132
University of Virginia, 125–127, 132, 141
University of Wisconsin-Green Bay (UWGB), ix, 106–111, 123–124, 142–144
University of Wisconsin-Madison, 132
Utopianism, 40–43, 48

Veterans, 83–86
Vietnam War, 29, 44–46, 80, 86, 115, 117, 140

Wall Street Journal, 20
Wallis, Jim, 5, 75
Walter, Lynn, xi, 123
Warach, Eli, 85, 152

Washington, D.C., 5, 25–28, 32, 37
Washington Post, xii, xiv, 19, 74
Weber, Eugen, 78
Weber, Max, 52, 144
Weekly Standard, 67
Weidner, Edward, 106
Welfare, 8, 12, 17, 26–27, 35, 53
West, Cornel, 5, 29, 40, 69
Whitman, Walt, 39
Will, George, 23
Wilson, Guy, 126
Winkler, Allan, 71

Wisconsin Labor History Society, xii
Wolfe, Alan, 5
Wolff, Edward, 8
Women's history, 71
Wood, Ellen Meiksins, 48
Working class, 8–10, 48, 80, 89–93
Writing, xv–xviii, 71–71, 104

Yale University, 132

Zilles, Michael, 143
Zinn, Howard, 80–82

Harvey J. Kaye is the Ben and Joyce Rosenberg Professor of Social Change and Development and Director of the Center for History and Social Change at the University of Wisconsin–Green Bay. He writes the World View column for *The Times Higher Education Supplement* and contributes regularly to *The Chronicle of Higher Education.* His many books include *The British Marxist Historians*, *The Education of Desire* (for which he received the 1993 Isaac Deutscher Memorial Prize), *The Powers of the Past*, *"Why Do Ruling Classes Fear History?" and Other Questions*, and *Thomas Paine: Firebrand of the Revolution.*

Frances Fox Piven is Distinguished Professor of Political Science and Sociology at the City University of New York Graduate Center and, with Richard Cloward, the author of *Regulating the Poor*, *The New Class War*, and *Breaking the Social Compact.*